ULTIMATE PURSUIT

LOVE GOD, LOVE PEOPLE

ENDORSEMENTS

Renny Bailey is a devoted follower of Christ and a gifted teacher. Her powerful testimony of salvation, deliverance, and redemption connects with people from all backgrounds. Her ability to weave the stories of her life as a disciple, wife, and mother with the message of the gospel has helped numerous people in our church and community discover God's plan for their lives. As members of Christian Chapel, I have watched Renny and Dan live with integrity as they seek to advance God's kingdom in the world. She authentically lives out her faith in seasons of joy and seasons of suffering. Her transparent story of God's grace will bring hope to all who hear it.
—**Chris Dow**, Lead Pastor, Christian Chapel, Tulsa, OK

In a life truly surrendered to the Lordship of Jesus, every aspect of one's past, present, and future can be used to glorify the King and reveal him to others so he may be seen and known as he truly is. This is what Renny Bailey does not only in her book but in her life.

Ultimate Pursuit delivers a powerful representation of Jesus and his unyielding desire for intimacy with each of us by expertly blending Scripture and the vulnerability of intimate personal testimony. The result is a compelling

presentation of the gospel that is encouraging, challenging, and beneficial for every believer at any stage in their walk with God."
—**Shane Bloedorn**, Sector Manager, Overland Missions-Chipepo, Zambia

In *Ultimate Pursuit*, Renny Bailey explains the hope-filled plan of God that will touch your heart and encourage you no matter your age. With incredible depth, her explanations delve beyond the surface and open up new understanding and insights. With words of truth, she clearly explains salvation's good news with compassion from her own walk with Christ, leading you toward a deeper relationship with Christ.
—**Kathy Key**, Bible teacher & life coach

In *Ultimate Pursuit*, Renny Bailey weaves together her personal experiences through rich storytelling, creating an engaging and inspiring read. Her authentic walk with Jesus shines through in every chapter, offering refreshing insights into what it means to truly love God and love others. Renny's practical yet powerful approach is grounded in the Word of God, and her message is rooted deeply in biblical truth. *Ultimate Pursuit* takes you on a heartfelt journey that will inspire and encourage you to pursue God with all your heart, soul, mind, and strength.
—**Amy Beiler**, Children's Pastor, Christian Chapel, Tulsa, OK

Having read *Ultimate Pursuit* by Renny Bailey, I was moved by her passion to experience life as God intended. She beautifully describes the life we should embrace as followers of Christ and provides practical ways on how we do that. If you have ever wondered what your purpose in life is, *Ultimate Pursuit* answers that question. We are here to love Christ with all our heart, soul, and might. As we do, Bailey explains how it generates passion to run our

race, fulfill our purpose, be transformed to become more like Christ, and love others well. The book is for anyone who wants to grow and experience more of the life Christ promises.
—**Mike Buie**, Associate Pastor, Christian Chapel, Tulsa, OK

God brought Renny into my life when I was searching for a way to be a better wife, mom, and person. I had accepted Jesus as my Savior but lacked the knowledge of how to give and live my life for him. Renny taught me how God's word applied to my everyday life. She helped me to understand what his word meant and how to look to his word for answers. Renny has an amazing testimony, and she uses that knowledge to counsel, disciple, and to show God's amazing love.

I am so excited for this book because I know that, through Renny's writing, her mentoring and teaching continue for me and the many readers that this book will bless.
—**Stacie Tutton**, former MOPS Leader

For over thirty years, Renny Bailey has served the body of Christ through the ministry of discipleship, mentoring, and Spirit-empowered Bible teaching. Drawing from her wealth of experience, her new book, *Ultimate Pursuit: Love God, Love People,* offers readers a user-friendly guide toward the development of Christian maturity. Rich in life metaphors, Scripture, and stories from her personal life, Bailey challenges all who would follow Jesus to not only receive new life in Christ, but to continue a life-long pursuit, enabling them to leave a legacy for those who will follow.

In this book, Renny offers helpful exhortations and the importance of walking with the Holy Spirit throughout our journey of faith.
—**R. Chene' Tucker**, MSW, LCSW, itinerant minister, therapist/life coach, Healing Oaks Coaching and Counseling

ULTIMATE PURSUIT

LOVE GOD, LOVE PEOPLE

RENNY BAILEY

ELK LAKE PUBLISHING INC.
PUBLISHING THE POSITIVE
Plymouth, Massachusetts
A Christian Company
ElkLakePublishingInc.com

COPYRIGHT NOTICE

Ultimate Pursuit: Love God, Love People

Cover and Interior Design: Kelly Artieri, Deb Haggerty
Editor(s): Susan K. Stewart, Judy Hagey, Deb Haggerty

PUBLISHED BY: Elk Lake Publishing, Inc., 35 Dogwood Drive, Plymouth, MA 02360, 2025

Library Cataloging Data

Names: Bailey, Renny (Renny Bailey)

Ultimate Pursuit: Love God, Love People / Renny Bailey

144 p. 23cm × 15cm (9in × 6 in.)

ISBN-13: 9798891344716 (paperback) | 9798891344723 (trade paperback) | 9798891344730 (e-book)

Key Words: Christian living greatest commandment Mk 12 30 31; Christian women's issues inspiration faith gospel; Biblical wisdom personal growth prayer forgiveness; Self-help relationship with God Bible empowerment; Women spirituality love God others Mark 12 30 31; Christian living spiritual growth Jesus testimony; Christian women love the Lord life guidance faith

Library of Congress Control Number: 2025xxxxxx Nonfiction

DEDICATION

To my husband Dan—outside of Christ, I have no relationship that means more to me. It has been my absolute joy to run this race with you. You have yoked yourself with God to open up the way for this season of life. You have my most profound respect, love, and devotion.

To each of my Bailey/Bloedorn and ever-increasing tribe, thank you for your grace, challenges, and love throughout the years. Each of you has a unique part in my movement towards Christ's likeness. You have my heart, and I will be forever grateful.

To my dear friend, Marty Groenewold. Your faithful dedication to daily prayer and consistent encouragement has carried me across the finish line of this book. Our ever-deepening friendship has been a delightful surprise and a cherished gift.

In Mark 12:30-31, Jesus gives us the ultimate pursuit of our existence and provides the foundation to build our lives, "And you must love the Lord your God with all your heart, all your soul, all your mind, and all your strength.' The second is equally important: 'Love your neighbor as yourself.' No other commandment is greater than these."

TABLE OF CONTENTS

1. Keep the Main Thing the Main Thing
2. The Clear Directive
3. The Art of Living Well
4. The Most Important Commandment
5. The Way of Salvation
6. The Greatest Need of Humanity
7. Born from Above
8. A New Kind of Life
9. Legacy
10. The Development of Endurance
11. The Necessity of Endurance
12. Running to Win
13. The Heavenly prize
14. The Gift of Time
15. The Life of Faith
16. The Promise of No Condemnation
17. Caught in the Web
18. The Source of All Comfort
19. The Ripple Effect
20. The Power of Dignity
21. The Advocate
22. The Fellowship of the Holy Spirit

INTRODUCTION

From the moment I stepped out of the darkness and into the light of Christ's kingdom, I have experienced the urgency to pursue wholeness—the kind of transformation that comes from loving God wholeheartedly in every dimension of my life. (Mark 12:30–31)

I have never been satisfied to run this race alone. At the prompting of the Holy Spirit, I have continually encouraged those around me to press in and take hold of all that Jesus obtained for us through the cross.

Thirty-five years later, this pursuit still lies at the core of my life.

Now, more than ever, I have seen a need for encouragement, inspiration, and support—as moments of ministry are filled with reminders of the true purpose of our life journey, according to Scripture. Never before have I poured out words of hope and comfort as I remind disheartened believers who are hurting and tired of the prize at the end of our running course—or to encourage those who don't yet know Christ to receive his beautiful invitation to eternal life.

Ultimate Pursuit is a collection of these messages. Each chapter is designed to build a solid foundation of hope and encouragement. I pray they will assist you in the ultimate pursuit of your life.

CHAPTER ONE:
KEEP THE MAIN THING THE MAIN THING

> But seek first his kingdom and his righteousness, and all these things will be given to you as well.
> (Matthew 6:33 NIV)

The full wording of this expression is: "The main thing is keeping the main thing the main thing."[1] Stephen Covey popularized this phrase in his book, *The Seven Habits of Highly Effective People.*

I think we can all agree this is a great idea. I believe we would also admit maintaining our focus is not easy to do. We don't simply drift into this mindset; focus takes purpose and intention. I would go so far as to say identifying the main thing that drives us can be difficult.

Though Mr. Covey coined the phrase, God presented this idea long ago throughout the Scriptures. One such place is found in Matthew 6:33. "But seek first his kingdom and his righteousness, and all these things will be given to you as well." (NIV)

Let's begin with verse 25 to gain a detailed understanding of this passage.

> Therefore I tell you, do not worry about your life, what you will eat or drink; or about your body, what you will wear. Is not life more than food and the body more than

> clothes? Look at the birds of the air; they do not sow or reap or store away in barns, and yet your heavenly Father feeds them. Are you not far more valuable than they? Can any one of you, by worrying, add a single hour to your life?
>
> And why do you worry about clothes? See how the flowers of the field grow. They do not labor or spin. Yet I tell you that not even Solomon, in all his splendor, was dressed like one of these. If that is how God clothes the grass of the field, which is here today and tomorrow is thrown into the fire, will he not much more clothe you—you of little faith? So do not worry, saying, 'What shall we eat?' or 'What shall we drink?' or 'What shall we wear?' For the pagans run after all these things, and your heavenly Father knows that you need them. But seek first his Kingdom and his righteousness, and all these things will be given to you as well. (Matthew 6:25–33 NIV)

These words of Jesus fall right in the middle of his Sermon on the Mount. He is speaking to a large crowd, primarily those living in poverty.

These words lack impact and understanding for us today. Most of us have never had to worry about what we eat, drink, or wear—at least not to the extent this specific group of people did.

To comprehend the weight of Jesus's teaching, we must recognize these basic needs were a daily reality for this crowd. Water and food were scarce, and most people had only one set of clothes. When Christ delivered these words, he faced a crowd where survival was an everyday concern. They spent their days preoccupied with these matters.

Food, drink, or clothing may not be a basic necessity in our culture, but we also have essential needs. We have financial concerns, career difficulties, health problems, prodigal children, and a vast array of fears that continually want to take up residency in our minds.

Some of us may want to scream, "Why not?" when we repeatedly hear Jesus telling us not to worry or be filled with anxiety. There are legitimate needs for living in this world. These words are difficult to hear, just like they were for the crowd Christ was preaching to.

The main point of this passage is this: Jesus wants us to be free from anxiety and worry. The question is, do we believe it is possible? I want to make it clear I am not speaking of a medical diagnosis of anxiety. I am referring to the anxiousness stemming from the stresses of living in this world.

In this section of Scripture, Jesus addresses worry six times and provides eight arguments or reasons why we do not need to live a life consumed by fear. He doesn't just command us not to be anxious; he supports this command and shows us how we can live without fear.

In verse 33, our Lord gives us the solution to obtaining our freedom: Seek the kingdom of God first.

Jesus invites us to live the kingdom life intentionally. He is inviting you and me to apply what we believe practically. He instructs us to disrupt the constant flow of anxiety the world wants to burden us with and focus on this one thing: the pursuit of the kingdom of God.

Other passages throughout Scripture reveal a similar theme. If we do this one thing in life, everything else will fall into place. Isaiah 26:3: "You will keep in perfect peace, all who trust in you, all whose thoughts are fixed on you!"

In Psalm 23:1, we read, "The Lord is my shepherd; I have all that I need." When we make Jesus our shepherd, our needs will be met. In Matthew 6:10–11, Jesus teaches us how to pray. "May your Kingdom come soon. May your will be done on earth, as it is in heaven. Give us today the food we need." We pray for the kingdom of God to come and then receive our daily bread.

Throughout the Scriptures, God repeatedly reveals what our priorities in life should be.

When we submit our lives to Christ, we begin a journey of learning to trust and live in his kingdom. This means we depend upon Christ for the entirety of our lives.

Jesus tells us in Matthew 6:33 to "seek" the kingdom of God. To seek something means to be wholly absorbed in the search. Have you ever lost your child? If so, you know the panic that overwhelms you. All of a sudden, everything else becomes second place. All else fades to the background. Finding your child is the only thing you can focus on.

Seeking is fundamental to our walk with Christ. Scripture commands us to seek God and his kingdom. Hebrews 11:6 declares that God rewards those who sincerely seek him and give all their passion and strength to pursuing him.

What we seek or run after reveals who we are. In John chapter 1, John the Baptist identifies Jesus, and two of John's disciples follow him. Our Lord stops and asks them who they are seeking and what they want.

God lets us choose what we will pursue. He allows us to follow our wants and desires. Our creator enables us to select the places where we invest our time and energy and the thoughts we allow to consume us; that's why we must seek the kingdom. He also tells us if we seek his kingdom, we will find it. Jeremiah 29:13 confirms this: "If you look for me wholeheartedly, you will find me."

We were created to follow God and acknowledge his presence in everything. This is the foundation of the greatest commandment. We are designed to pursue him wholeheartedly. This pursuit pulls the rest of our lives together. What we seek becomes primary in life, and everything else falls into place behind that priority.

Seeking God's kingdom first creates the capacity for everything else to follow. This provides unique avenues for

Christ to meet our needs. Most often, he chooses to meet these needs through those around us.

Jesus sums up his teaching with these words from Matthew 6:34, "So don't worry about tomorrow, for tomorrow will bring its own worries. Today's trouble is enough for today." We're to stay focused on the twenty-four hours we live in. To be fully present to those we do life with. Jesus tells us that tomorrow will take care of itself; he has provided enough grace for today.

Lamentations 3:23 tells us God's grace and mercy are available and fresh every single morning.

A quote frequently attributed to Corrie Ten Boom always brings into focus for me the necessity of keeping my eyes on Jesus. "Worrying is carrying tomorrow's load with today's strength—carrying two days at once. It is moving into tomorrow ahead of time. Worrying doesn't empty tomorrow of its sorrow; it empties today of its strength and possibilities."

CHAPTER TWO: THE CLEAR DIRECTIVE

> The second is equally important: Love your neighbor as yourself.
> (Mark 12:31)

In Mark 12:28–30, Jesus articulates the greatest commandment. We are directed to have wholehearted love for God—a love that consumes every human aspect. In verse 31, Christ tells us the second commandment is equally important: we are to love our neighbor as we love ourselves.

With these two verses, our Lord dismisses the Jewish tradition of the detailed ranking of the many laws. He informs them only two things are necessary: loving God and loving their neighbor.

In Matthew's recording of this conversation, we read in 22:40, "The entire law and all the demands of the prophets are based on these two commandments." Christ reveals that all laws and commands are achieved when these two directives are fully satisfied.

The law and the prophets refer to the entire Old Testament. The law refers to the books of Moses: Genesis, Exodus, Leviticus, Numbers, and Deuteronomy. The prophets include the rest of the Old Testament. The Jewish people considered all writers of Scripture to be prophets.

Jesus did not come to abolish the law but to fulfill it. John 1:45 says, "Philip found Nathanael and told him, 'We have found the one Moses wrote about in the Law, and about whom the prophets also wrote—Jesus of Nazareth, the son of Joseph.'" (NIV) Philip believed Jesus had met all the criteria of the Old Testament.

As I studied the Scriptures, I discovered these two commandments cannot be separated. We can discuss each one individually, but we cannot separate them in principle. The following are four portions of Scripture that reveal the unity of these commands.

1 John 2:9, "If anyone claims, 'I am living in the light,' but hates a fellow believer, that person is still living in darkness."

1 John 3:16–18, "We know what real love is because Jesus gave up his life for us. So, we also ought to give up our lives for our brothers and sisters. If someone has enough money to live well and sees a brother or sister in need but shows no compassion—how can God's love be in that person? Dear children, let's not merely say that we love each other; let us show the truth by our actions."

1 John 4:7–8, "Dear friends, let us continue to love one another, for love comes from God. Anyone who loves is a child of God and knows God. But anyone who does not love does not know God, for God is love."

1 John 4:20–21, "If someone says, 'I love God,' but hates a fellow believer, that person is a liar; for if we don't love people we can see, how can we love God, whom we cannot see? And he has given us this command: Those who love God must also love their fellow believers."

From these Scriptures, we can only conclude loving others is grounded in the first commandment. Loving your neighbor is a natural development that comes from a wholehearted love for God. Placing all our affection on Christ will transition us to a love for people. As we grow in our ability to love our Father with all aspects of our humanity, loving others will be an extension of our affection for Jesus.

Reflecting on my life journey, I have concluded where these two commands intersect has been the point of my most profound transformation. My struggle to let go of self-focus and move toward Christlikeness originated in this essential space. I believe this is God's intention for each of us.

When I began my journey with Jesus and experienced his unconditional love, I couldn't take my focus off him. I was consumed with wanting to know and love him with everything I had. Staying anchored in this place of deep connection initiated an intense inner transformation, which is the intention of the gospel.

At that point, those who knew me and were observing my life could see very little external change. Blatant areas of sin were still evident. Learning to love God with all my heart, soul, mind, and strength began deep inside me and developed over time. The progression of time is necessary for lasting change.

When we hear the word self-love, we often become uncomfortable. Regarding love for oneself, society frequently categorizes us into one of two positions. On one extreme, self-love is considered an inflated sense of self-importance. At the other end of the spectrum, we may be applauded for working aggressively to obtain all that we desire.

When Christ tells us to love others as we love ourselves, there is an undertone of assumption. He doesn't command us to love ourselves. The clear directive is to love others as we love ourselves. I perceive it as something our creator already knows about us. We are all born with a powerful predisposition towards self-preservation. This tendency is part of our humanity.

We all want to live a good life with all our needs met each day. We want to be protected from the violence in the world around us. We have a deep longing for intimate relationships. We have a desire to be healthy and strong. We are already given to self-love.

In this clear directive from Jesus, the word "as" means "in the same way." Understanding this definition brings clarity to what Jesus is saying: as we nurture and care for our lives, we should not forget to look up and outward to our neighbor, who is also trying to do the same.

I recall the earliest parts of my journey with Christ as a new believer and a new single mom. I had many needs. As I exerted energy and effort toward all the things that come under the umbrella of self-love, without any exaggeration, I can say Christ met every one of those needs. As he provided for me, my vision expanded outside myself.

If we focus on Christ to meet the necessities of life and allow him to fulfill the desire to live a life of significance, our relationship with Jesus will fully satisfy our hearts, souls, and minds. This is the point of transformation of self-love. As we become confident in God's provision and care and grow in our love for our Lord, we will lift our eyes and look outward to those around us.

From this deep well of intimacy with our creator, loving our neighbors as we love ourselves becomes the observable expression and practical fulfillment of loving God. Our love for our Father is visible when we practically and sacrificially love others.

How we love demonstrates who we are. When we love others well, we reveal the gospel and the transformational power of the cross.

John 13:35, "Your love for one another will prove to the world that you are my disciples."

CHAPTER THREE: THE ART OF LIVING WELL

> And you must love the Lord your God with all your heart, all your soul, all your mind, and all your strength. (Mark 12:30)

One of our strongest desires is to create a meaningful existence. Deep in our DNA, we are wired to desire a life that matters.

In Genesis 1:26–28, God reveals he has created us in his image. God gave Adam and Eve dominion over the earth. They were to rule, reign, and accomplish God's earthly purposes. This longing to make a difference is evidence of God's image within us.

The description of a significant life may vary from person to person, but the desire to live well is the driving force beneath the many layers of our existence.

This life we live is not a practice run. We don't receive the opportunity for a do-over to see if we can perform at a higher level. Life is not the ACT, where you can repeat the exam to improve your score. Remember those? I searched on the internet and found you can now take the assessment up to twelve times. Most students attempt the test at least two or three times and can improve their scores.[1]

Life doesn't work that way. We get one shot. And if we just get one opportunity to live well, wouldn't we be wise to turn to the one who created us? We should seek out God's intentions and expectations for this one life we live.

As followers of Jesus, we must possess knowledge to understand our spiritual lives. Such wisdom is essential to our journey of living well. We live synergistically with God; our lives are an existence lived through interaction with our Father through prayer, worship, listening, and reading his Word.

But let's be honest. With the many distractions surrounding us, becoming aware of God's presence can be a challenge. A frenzy of activity assaults us from every direction, every minute of our day. Endless to-do lists and obligations continually pull on our lives, leaving little room for anything else.

Within the Christian community, we often experience a staggering sense of never-ending agendas. The internet and publications are filled with the perfect Bible plans, the best podcasts, and the top practices to incorporate into our daily lives.

Overwhelmed by life, our question to Jesus can be much like that of the scribe we find in Matthew 22:36–37 who asks, "Teacher, which is the most important commandment in the law of Moses? Jesus replied, 'You must love the Lord your God with all your heart, all your soul, and all your mind.'"

When Mark (12:28–31) and Luke (10:27) record these words of Jesus, they add the word "strength." Mark 12:28–31 says:

> One of the teachers of religious law was standing there listening to the debate. He realized Jesus had answered well, so he asked, "Of all the commandments, which is the most important?' Jesus replied, 'The most important commandment is this: 'Listen, O Israel! The Lord our God is the one and only Lord. And you must love the Lord your God with all your heart, all your soul, all

> your mind, and all your strength.' The second is equally important: 'Love your neighbor as yourself." No other commandment is greater than these.

A "teacher of religious law" is also referenced in Scripture as a scribe or lawyer. These teachers of the law were primarily Pharisees, known as authorities on religious law. Their specialty was defining the application of commands through their biblical interpretations.

Remember the teacher of religious law or scribe? He asked Jesus, "Of all the commandments, which is the most important?"

He is not asking which commandment God gave first. He asks a question of priority. He wants to know at the primary level: What's the bottom line here? What is the most essential command God has ever given the world?

At first glance, this inquiry appears straightforward. However, to the student of Scripture, the question contains a vital implication.

The Jewish religious system created 613 laws from the Decalogue or Ten Commandments. Since the Ten Commandments have 613 letters in the Hebrew language, the Jewish religious system determined there had to be a total of 613 statutes.

According to tradition, all 613 laws—with the Ten Commandments leading—were drawn from the Torah, also known as the Books of Moses. The Old Testament's first five books Moses wrote are also known as the Pentateuch: Genesis, Exodus, Leviticus, Numbers, and Deuteronomy.

These ordinances were then divided into two categories. The Jewish leaders determined that 248 were considered positive—do this/do that—and 365 were considered negative—don't do this/don't do that. Debating over the priority of specific laws was a routine part of the rabbinical dialogue.

Their arguments circled the question of which command was so central to the others that all the rest orbited around this single command. Jesus cut right to the chase. He responded immediately which was not typical for him; he often answered a question with a question, especially when challenged.

He quickly sums up all 613 commandments with one word: love. Love God and love people.

When Matthew shares this portion of Scripture, he gives us more of the conversation. In verse 22:40, Jesus tells the scribe: "The entire law and all the demands of the prophets are based on these two commandments."

Jesus directed the leader's attention to the idea that his answer was connected to the Ten Commandments. The first four commands are about loving God, and commandments five through ten are about loving humankind. The first four commandments concern our vertical relationship to God. The last six address the horizontal relationship of human to human.

These two commands are a summary of the whole law. In one moment, Jesus brings it all together and simplistically defines the most important commandment: love God and love others.

The religious leadership had strapped the Jewish people with hundreds of rules and regulations to follow. Let that soak in. We cannot imagine the cloud of weariness the Jewish people lived under—the hopelessness they must have experienced in trying to fulfill the Jewish religious law.

In Matthew 11:28, Jesus addresses this religious exhaustion: "Then Jesus said, 'Come to me, all of you who are weary and carry heavy burdens, and I will give you rest.'"

Jesus revealed to the scribe no commandment is greater than to love God with all our heart, soul, mind, and strength. Without hesitation, Jesus gave this scribe and all humanity the ultimate pursuit of our lives. Reaching for and pursuing this command directs the trajectory of life.

CHAPTER FOUR: THE MOST IMPORTANT COMMANDMENT

> One of the teachers of religious law stood, listening to the debate. He realized Jesus had answered well, so he asked, "Of all the commandments, which is the most important?"
> (Mark 12:28)

To understand the depth of the scribe's question and the power behind Jesus's answer, we must look at the context of this conversation in Mark. Understanding the context helps us comprehend the question.

The setting in Mark 12 takes place in Jerusalem during Passion Week, also known as Holy Week. This is the week Christ was arrested, crucified, and raised from the dead. The conversation occurs on Wednesday. On the previous Monday, Jesus made his triumphal entry into Jerusalem. On Tuesday, he clears the temple area of everyone using the house of worship as a marketplace. Christ calls the temple a "den of thieves" (Mark 11:17).

Thursday is the scene of the Last Supper, and he will be crucified on Friday. This timing is important. Jesus is just a few days from his crucifixion; he chooses his words carefully. He understands his time on earth is coming to an end.

Jesus leads with the bedrock of the greatest commandment, "The Lord our God is the one and only Lord" (Mark 12:29).

We must consider the world and culture at the time Jesus made this radical declaration to love and commit to only one God. The Israelites were the only people who worshipped one God. Every other people group worshipped multiple gods. Only Israel sanctioned this monotheistic belief.

In the series of questions, this is the Pharisee's third and final attempt to trap Jesus, to tempt him to say something that will force the people to turn against him. The Pharisees were afraid of Jesus's growing popularity.

Christ's fame threatened the power of these holy men, which in turn, threatened their income. And they envied Jesus because the people loved him. His growing approval exposed the Pharisees on all levels.

According to Mark 12:28, "One of the teachers of religious law was standing there listening to the debate. He realized that Jesus had answered well, so he asked, 'Of all the commandments, which is the most important?'"

The Scripture suggests a previous occasion where the scribe watched and listened to an exchange of questions and answers. Jesus was interrogated twice, leading up to the scribe's question. The teacher of the law perceives Jesus's replies to the investigation as astonishing. He is intrigued by Jesus's responses.

The first confrontation in this series of questions centers on the controversial issue of paying taxes to Rome. The Pharisees and Herodians (a political party that followed Herod) confront Jesus. He gives a wise answer. He tells them, "Give to Caesar what belongs to Caesar, and give to God what belongs to God" (Mark 12:17).

Christ stays clear of the trap they have set for him.

The second confrontation is by the Sadducees. Their goal is to entrap Jesus regarding his views on the resurrection. The Sadducees did not believe in an afterlife or any type of resurrection. Neither did they believe in angels, which Jesus addresses in his answer to them.

The Sadducees asked Jesus a bizarre and hypothetical question about resurrection life and one they believe to be unanswerable. For all intents and purposes, they were not asking Jesus a question. They are trying to prove him wrong. Christ counters with verse 24: "Your mistake is that you don't know the Scriptures, and you don't know the power of God" (Mark 12:18–27).

The Lord's response fueled their hostility and hatred toward him.

The Pharisees felt Jesus had just answered the Sadducees well. They heard Jesus correct the Sadducees on their view of resurrection life in a direct manner. He silenced them and put them in their place.

They knew Jesus's answers were exceptional and accurate.

In my research for this book, I was startled by the number of Scriptures that revealed the Jewish leaders recognized Jesus as authoritative and precise in his teachings. Following is a sample of their responses to Christ's answers.

Matthew 2:22: "His reply amazed them, and they went away."

Matthew 22:33: "When the crowds heard him, they were astounded at his teaching."

Matthew 22:46: "No one could answer him. And after that, no one dared to ask him any more questions."

Mark 12:17: "His reply completely amazed them."

Mark 12:26: "So they failed to trap him by what he said in front of the people. Instead, they were amazed by his answer, and they became silent."

The Pharisees and Sadducees' attempts to trap Jesus only created a more significant platform to showcase the brilliance of Christ. And yet, they pursued their plot to see Jesus executed. I find this difficult to comprehend.

Neither question was an attempt to understand the Scriptures more fully. They were not authentic questions asked to attain real answers. Rather, the religious leaders set up the inquests to trap and humiliate Jesus.

As the scribe in Mark 12:28 approaches Jesus, he brings a different atmosphere. In the tone of his conversation, we don't perceive sarcasm or sense any hostility towards Christ. He was authentically impressed with how our Lord has handled the Pharisees and Sadducees.

The teacher, also a Pharisee, according to Matthew 22:25, knew what the religious leaders were up to in their questioning and knew Jesus had given clever and thoughtful answers.

Mark 12:28 informs us: "He realized Jesus had answered well ..." Through the scribe's response, we understand he genuinely wants to learn something. He takes the opportunity to probe Jesus's thoughts on an honest question.

At the same time, we need to acknowledge he is trying to trap Jesus. Matthew 22:35–36 explains: "One of them, an expert in religious law, tried to trap him with this question: 'Teacher, which is the most important commandment in the law of Moses?'"

The scribe's inquiry is also a question both the Pharisees and the Sadducees could approve. They are united in their desire to trap Jesus and hope he will give an answer outside the law of Moses.

The Pharisees studied the Old Testament and all their interpretations of the Scriptures, as well as the traditions developed around it, and claimed this as their law. They held the position that Jesus's teachings contradicted their commands. They believed them to be against Moses and the Old Testament law.

On the other hand, the Sadducees only considered the books of Moses to be from God. The scribe asks, "What is the greatest commandment?"

Jesus cleverly reaches back into the past and answers from a framework both the Pharisees and the Sadducees can agree upon—the books of Moses.

He begins with, "Hear O Israel, the Lord is One." Jesus' statement was an expected reply, a Jewish answer. Christ's response comes directly from a Jewish prayer known as the Shema. From the time of Jesus until now, the Orthodox Jews recite this prayer daily.

The benediction is comprised of passages of Scripture from Deut. 6:4–9, 11:13–21, and Numbers 15:37–41. The Shema is the Jewish statement of faith, meaning "to listen or to hear and obey." In Hebrew, there is no word for obey, so when written, obey and hear are interchangeable.

This understanding makes the word Shema powerful.

When Jesus references the Shema, he conveys the idea of listening and doing. We must understand hearing the words of Christ is not enough. He is commanding us to put them into action.

God's intention was never for us to read his words now and again. He doesn't want us to treat the Bible like an entertaining children's story. His design was for us to dig deep into the riches of his words and to apply them to our life circumstances.

In my time with Jesus, studying and meditating on these words in Mark 12:28–31, I have come to an understanding that shakes me to the core of my being. This mandate from our Lord was not just for Israel then or the Christian community now. Rather, it is for the entire world, today, tomorrow, and forever.

Christ's command summarizes the whole obligation of human beings before their creator. Yes, this directive defines us as believers. We are those who love God with all our human abilities. But this charge Jesus speaks across the generations also separates humankind into only two categories: those who love God and those who don't.

Disobedience to this command brings about divine eternal judgment and far-reaching implications.

As our understanding of this deepens, we land on the bedrock of comprehending why Jesus, just a few days from his crucifixion, tells his followers in verse 31, "No other commandment is greater than these."

CHAPTER FIVE:
THE WAY OF SALVATION

> You were jarred into turning things around.
> (2 Corinthians 7:8-10 MSG)

When we engage our hearts and minds in the New Testament Scriptures, especially the four Gospels, we get a glimpse of a different world.

I'm not referring to cultural or historical differences. Within the pages of the New Testament, we read story after story of ordinary people who enter a relationship with Christ. And we observe a radical change in their lives.

The believer's new nature gives way to a transformed belief structure with a new view of life. We become spectators, as personalities once harsh and cruel yield to compassion and love.

As we survey the lives of Peter, Matthew, Paul, and many others, we can't help but notice the extreme contrast between their lives before Christ and after Christ. However, when we look within our own lives and examine our own experiences, we seldom observe a significant difference.

And yet, throughout the New Testament, the vision presented is distinct and clear: entry into the kingdom of God (the new birth) brings radical transformation. Our salvation changes the trajectory of life's story.

Throughout my journey, I've encountered many who have experienced harsh circumstances, disappointments, addictions, and extreme difficulties in marriage and parenting roles. I have observed many who lost hope that change is possible. But the evidence found in the New Testament demonstrates pronounced differences through Christ is indeed possible for all of us.

Not only is it possible, but transformation is the intention of the gospel.

So, how do we obey Jesus's command to love God with our heart, soul, mind, and strength (Mark 12:30)? Christ instructs us to love God with every dimension of our humanity. Where do we find the strategy to accomplish this command?

Let me answer these two essential questions by sharing a portion of my journey and what I have found to be true.

I was in a horrible car accident the night before my thirty-first birthday. A three-quarter-ton truck ran a red light at 45 mph and T-boned me. The truck hit me hard and bounced off my car and struck me two more times.

My two little boys—ages two and four at the time—and an eighteen-month-old girl I cared for were in the back seat. They were okay but were frightened and experienced only minor bruises. The first responders needed the jaws of life to remove me from our car.

I had a fractured neck, a closed head injury, nine fractured ribs, a collapsed lung, a fractured arm, and a pelvic fracture. I was in the ICU for five days and spent twenty-one days in the hospital.

Not only was I physically broken, I was spiritually and emotionally broken as well. My body's intense physical pain reflected the distress in my heart. The brokenness and vulnerability I encountered in my body brought the deep anguish in my soul to the surface.

I was depressed, angry, and covered with layers of shame. In the middle of a divorce, I was confronted by experiences in my past that had been dormant. I felt like a failure as a wife, a mother, and a daughter. I knew God was out there, but I couldn't entirely lay hold of a life with him.

I slowly became aware of my environment in the darkened ICU. The noise of machines monitoring my vital signs filled the room. The hissing and crackling of the compression sleeves inflating and deflating kept me on edge. The tube that allowed my lung to expand generated a constant ache in my side.

As I stared at the ceiling, I was struck by the urgency of my situation. My mind knew something more intense was going on than the pain my body was experiencing. I felt vulnerable and lost. My arms ached to hold my boys—both to ground me and to reassure them—and to know they were okay.

The car wreck got my attention. It was as if I were coming out of a deep sleep and observing the devastation around me. Years later, I discovered words in 2 Corinthians 7:8–11 (MSG) that captured the way I felt at the moment.

In 1 Corinthians, Paul wrote a necessary but harsh letter to the Corinthians. He challenged them on their beliefs and actions within the church. As a more seasoned man, Paul's second letter is one of reconciliation.

Paul's words instructed and encouraged the recipients of his letter in 2 Corinthians 7:

> The letter upset you, but only for a while. Now I'm glad—not that you were upset, but that *you were jarred into turning things around*. You let the distress bring you to God, not drive you from him. The result was all gain, no loss.
>
> Distress that drives us to God does that. It turns us around. It gets us back in the way of salvation. We never

> regret that kind of pain. But those who let distress drive them away from God are full of regret and end up on a deathbed of regret.
>
> And now, isn't it wonderful all the ways in which this distress has goaded you closer to God? You're more alive, more concerned, more sensitive, more reverent, more human, more passionate, more responsible. Looked at from any angle, you've come out of this with purity of heart. (7:8–11 MSG emphasis added)

As I lay in the ICU that first night, I cried out to a God I had heard of all my life but had never really known. I gave my life to Christ, and I experienced a newness of life deep within me that is difficult to put into words. Second Corinthians 5:17 tells it best: "This means that anyone who belongs to Christ has become a new person. The old life is gone; a new life has begun!"

In other words, I was one way, and after I gave my life to Jesus, I was another way.

I was born into a religious family. I went to church on Sundays. I said my prayers. My parents did all they knew to do. Still, I didn't have a personal relationship with Jesus. I could not follow God vicariously through my parents' relationship with him.

Even though our families may follow Christ, we cannot inherit salvation. We need to make the personal and individual decision to be spiritually reborn.

I began to read the Bible found in my bedside table. As a nurse, I'd seen those bedside Bibles and often wondered if patients read them. Here I was, devouring the words written on the pages in front of me. My heart was coming alive. I was awakened from my deep slumber.

I had always loved to read. As a child and young adult, my appetite for books was insatiable. But up until that point in my life, I had never read the Bible. I never had the desire or was aware I needed to read the written Word of God.

I soon understood God was telling his story through the pages of Scripture—a story that began in eternity past and reaches deep into the future.

Merriam-Webster defines story as: "an account of incidents or events."[1] But the concept of story originated with God. Our Lord is the master storyteller, and he has chosen this idea of story to be the primary way he presents himself to us. We learn who our Father is through the stories in the Bible. The Word of God reflects his story. His Word is the predominant way he reveals himself to us. Scripture explains who he is and how to enter a relationship with him.

In antiquity, the story of God was passed on through the family and carried from one generation to the next through oral tradition. The Holy Scriptures are how God has chosen to preserve and pass on this knowledge. There is a purpose to God's story. The Bible is intended to impact and shape our lives. Christ invites you and me into his story.

When we observe Jesus's life in the four Gospels—Matthew, Mark, Luke, and John—we see God revealing truth through stories or parables. Parable comes from "parabolē," which suggests placing two things side by side for comparison. To help us better understand what Jesus is teaching, he uses a familiar idea contained in story form alongside an unfamiliar or new idea or truth. These stories help our minds, and our hearts connect to that truth.

Our lives are influenced by story.

At our first gasp of air, we are born into an unfolding storyline. Right here at this moment, you and I are living out a script determined by our decisions. And one day, we will pass our stories to the next generation.

The new birth is expected to alter our journey. Our encounter with the gospel of Christ is intended to impact and transform our story.

On May 21, 1990, the day of my accident, I was "jarred into turning things around." (2 Corinthians 7:8–10 MSG) I accepted Jesus's invitation and stepped into the story he had written just for me. The changes in my journey have been too numerous to count. But with each transformation, every movement toward wholeness has brought me closer to what Jesus calls the greatest commandment.

In Mark 12:30, Jesus instructs us to love God with all our heart, soul, mind, and strength. With these words, he provides us with a new storyline by which to live. But before we can live out the ultimate pursuit of our lives, we must first accept his invitation of salvation.

If you choose to accept God's gift, the master storyteller will rewrite your life journey. He will do so for everyone who receives his Son, Jesus Christ.

CHAPTER SIX: THE GREATEST NEED OF HUMANITY

> Jesus replied, "I tell you the truth, unless you are born again, you cannot see the Kingdom of God." (John 3:3)

The first chapter of Mike Petzer's book *The Gospel of Identity* begins with these words: "At the very beginning of Jesus's earthly ministry, he told a religious ruler named Nicodemus what the greatest need of man was. That man needed to be restored to the life that God had originally created him to be possessor of."[1]

I cringed the first time I heard the expression "born again."

A classmate from high school introduced me to the phrase. I was challenged and uncomfortable as I listened to her tell me she had been born again. I responded to my courageous friend with extreme rudeness. We had grown up together in the same religion, and this "born again" idea was a drastic departure from all I had known. Her words caused intense agitation deep within me. I have repeatedly seen this same agitation in others over the years of following Christ and sharing his gospel. A decade would pass until I fully understood the costly gift Christ had offered me through this relationship.

The term "born again" originated in a conversation between Jesus and a man named Nicodemus. We find this dialogue in John's Gospel, 3:1–17. Verse one presents us with this encounter: "Now there was a Pharisee, a man named Nicodemus who was a member of the Jewish ruling council" (NIV).

We need to understand who this man was to grasp the relevance of this conversation. This one sentence, packed with information, communicates the essence of Nicodemus.

Nicodemus was a Pharisee. The word Pharisee comes from a Hebrew word meaning "separated." The Pharisees' strict observance of the law and emphasis on personal holiness distinguished them. They were holy men devoted to the Scriptures. As a skilled theologian, Nicodemus was considered an expert in the law.

Verse one also informs us he was a member of the Jewish ruling council. The verse identifies Nicodemus as part of the Sanhedrin, the dominant presiding body for the Jewish people. This supreme court of ancient Israel consisted of seventy men and the high priest. Not all Pharisees were elevated to membership in the Sanhedrin. Such status placed Nicodemus in a significant position regarding the governmental affairs of the Jewish people.

John 3:2 tells us more. Nicodemus came to Jesus at night, but the Scriptures do not reveal why. Many theologians have speculated on several possible motives. As a member of the Sanhedrin, one of his duties would have been to question any teachers he felt were leading the people astray. Some theologians speculate Nicodemus was afraid to be seen with Jesus in broad daylight; maybe he was even embarrassed or ashamed.

But what Nicodemus says in John 3:2 is what grabs my attention. "Rabbi, we know that you are a teacher who has come from God. For no one could perform the signs you are doing if God were not with him."

Nicodemus esteems Jesus by using the title of Rabbi, which means "teacher" in Hebrew. He respectfully affirms and acknowledges Jesus as an authentic teacher, and one whom God sent. The phrase "we know" indicates he is also speaking for others. At this point, Nicodemus is confirming Jesus theologically and personally. His admiration towards Christ demonstrates the Pharisee's confidence in his position before God.

In John, Chapter 2, the disciple provides valuable information, which leads us into the conversation between Jesus and the Pharisee.

Our Lord is now in Jerusalem. He has just gone through the temple and has thrown everyone out. This is the first of two incidents in which Christ clears the temple. The first happens at the beginning of Jesus's ministry, and the second occurs at the end of his three-year ministry. The Jewish people dishonored God by turning the temple into a place of business. .

According to verse 23, Jesus is performing miracles visible to the crowds gathered for the annual Jewish festivals. They begin to believe in what Jesus is doing. John 2:23–25: "Because of the miraculous signs Jesus did in Jerusalem at the Passover celebration, many began to trust in him. But Jesus didn't trust them because he knew all about people. No one needed to tell him about human nature, for he knew what was in each person's heart."

Christ knew their belief wasn't saving faith; there was not enough substance.

Because of Nicodemus's words in John 3:2, "Rabbi, we know ..." we understand he is one of the many who believed. Interestingly, Jesus does not acknowledge Nicodemus's affirmations.

Our Lord, perceiving what was in Nicodemus's heart and knowing what was on his mind, directly begins to teach him. John 3:3, "Very truly I tell you, no one can see the kingdom of God unless they are born again."

John leaves no doubt in the readers' minds that Nicodemus is a religious and devout man. He has spent the entirety of his adult life studying the Scriptures. He is educated, has no financial needs, and has obtained significant status among the Jewish people. In John 3:4, we also see that Nicodemus is advanced in age. He asks Jesus how an old man can return to his mother's womb and be born again.

Jesus tells this devout, moral, and elderly man nothing he has done will allow him into the kingdom of God. We would have been hard-pressed to find a more devout and traditionally ethical person. So, Jesus's demand to be born again was not a call to become more religious.

After the incident with my school friend, I frequently heard the term born again. As I surveyed the culture around me, I found the response to the phrase was almost always critical and derogatory, often connected to someone who was extremely broken and had a shattered life. To be born again implied someone broken had found Jesus and gone off the deep end.

Little did I know I would fall into this category years later.

As we study John 3, we learn Nicodemus does not need an emotional crutch. He isn't a broken, emotional man. His life appears stable. Life is going well for him. And still, Jesus tells him he must be born again. Jesus breaks all the stereotypes.

As a Pharisee, a layer of religious pride and arrogance covered this man's life. In Matthew 23:1–39, Jesus provides us with harsh criticisms of the Pharisees. He draws attention to their hypocrisy by illustrating their extreme lack of congruence between their inner being and outward actions.

In verses 1–5, Jesus tells the crowds and his disciples, "The teachers of religious law and the Pharisees are the official interpreters of the law of Moses. So practice and obey whatever they tell you, but don't follow their example. For they don't practice what they teach. They crush people with their unbearable religious demands and never lift a finger to ease the burden. Everything they do is for show."

In 23:27, Jesus delivers an unforgettable analogy, drawing attention to the Pharisees' religious fraud. "What sorrow awaits you teachers of religious law and you Pharisees. Hypocrites! For you are like whitewashed tombs—beautiful on the outside but filled on the inside with dead people's bones and all sorts of impurity."

Graves in the time of Jesus were frequently painted with white lime. A newly whitewashed tomb would be bright and clean-looking. The tombs were regularly decorated to draw attention to the grave. The image Jesus details was an extreme contrast to the contents of the burial chamber.

As humans, we like what's familiar and comfortable. We're hesitant to leave a way of life behind, even if we are sure that to do so would be to follow God's leading. Fear and possible rejection become traveling companions as we face the battle within our hearts.

My new life began to unfold, and I began to study the words of Jesus, I was confronted with an uncomfortable reality. Jesus was the one who said a person must be born again. He calls our attention to something necessary for every human being on earth.

We must first be reborn to obey the Great Commandment that Christ gives us in Mark 12:30. An analogy that helps bring this truth into focus is the concept of fire. Oxygen is an absolute requirement to create fire. If there is no oxygen, there is no fire.

Spiritual rebirth connects us to God; it is the only way to obtain the desire and perseverance to love the one true God with all our human ability.

CHAPTER SEVEN: BORN FROM ABOVE

> Jesus replied, "I assure you, no one can enter the Kingdom of God without being born of water and the Spirit. Humans can reproduce only human life, but the Holy Spirit gives birth to spiritual life. So don't be surprised when I say, 'You must be born again.'"
> (John 3:5–7)

In my early adult years of working as a registered nurse, I concluded there was no more tremendous privilege than to be present at the birth of a child or at the bedside of someone in their moment of death.

As grandparents of fourteen grandchildren, my husband and I have celebrated each new life added to our rich and growing legacy. Each child, marked with distinctive and beautiful memories, creates a significant space on our timeline.

The most recent addition is our granddaughter, Selah Kate.

Our son and daughter-in-law are missionaries to Zambia, Africa. They lived with us for eight years when they would return to the States for rest, reconnection with their church family, and having babies. Their calling as missionaries and sharing our home has given our family unique and memorable experiences. One such experience was my introduction to home births.

When the time came for Selah to enter our world, her birthing team was en route, but this little girl was not waiting on anyone. As I received my granddaughter into my arms and returned her to her mother, I was overwhelmed by the beauty and wonder surrounding this moment.

My newborn granddaughter was incredible to behold.

As extraordinary as the births of our children and grandchildren are, there remains something fundamentally wrong with each new life that enters this world. Scripture validates this in Psalm 51:5: "For I was born a sinner—yes, from the moment my mother conceived me," and again in Romans 3:10: "As the Scriptures say, 'No one is righteous—not even one.'"

Jesus authenticates this in John 3:6–7: "Humans can reproduce only human life, but the Holy Spirit gives birth to spiritual life. So don't be surprised when I say, 'You must be born again.'"

The Gospel of John was originally written in Greek. The word translated as "again" has two primary meanings. The first meaning conveys the idea of being born a second time but also holds the meaning of being born from above or, in the fullest sense, born of God.

Later in John 3:31, we see this reference about being born from above: "He has come from above and is greater than anyone else. We are of the earth, and we speak of earthly things, but he has come from heaven and is greater than anyone else."

This phrase, "born from above" refers to heaven, where God is. Jesus has come down from above, from another world, and has entered the human race.

Christ leaves no room for doubt in his dialogue with Nicodemus. He must be reborn from above to see and enter the kingdom of God. Without the rebirth, he remains outside the kingdom.

Our Lord tells this holy man and all of humanity we need more than a natural birth. We need to be born supernaturally. We require a fresh start—a birth from another dimension, another kingdom.

The second birth has nothing to do with this world. Nicodemus's status, traditions, lineage, or religious activities would not suffice for the new birth. The birth from above can only be produced by the Spirit of God. First Peter 1:3 explains, "All praise to God, the Father of our Lord Jesus Christ. It is by his great mercy we have been born again because God raised Jesus Christ from the dead."

This kingdom is a domain where Christ creates and recreates his people, giving his followers a new mind, heart, and destiny. Paul describes this in 2 Corinthians 5:17: "This means that anyone who belongs to Christ has become a new person. The old life is gone; a new life has begun."

In the Old Testament, Christ proclaims the principles of conversion and spiritual life through the prophet Ezekiel. In 36:25–27, he explains, "Then I will sprinkle clean water on you, and you will be clean. Your filth will be washed away, and you will no longer worship idols. And I will give you a new heart, and I will put a new spirit in you. I will take out your stony, stubborn heart and give you a tender, responsive heart. And I will put my Spirit in you so that you will follow my decrees and be careful to obey my regulations."

The New Testament consistently reveals that every person born on planet Earth is born spiritually dead. To be spiritually dead means to be separated from God. In Genesis, we learn that because of his disobedience, Adam ushered in sin and death for all humanity.

We may have existence, but we are born spiritually lifeless. We are incapable of doing anything to save ourselves.

Ephesians 2:1–3 is one of the most fascinating portions of Scripture, and it describes our spiritual condition before

Christ: "Once you were dead because of your disobedience and your many sins. You used to live in sin, just like the rest of the world, obeying the devil—the commander of the powers in the unseen world. He is the spirit at work in the hearts of those who refuse to obey God. All of us lived that way, following the passionate desires and inclinations of our sinful nature. By our very nature, we were subject to God's anger, just like everyone else."

This passage describes believers as once spiritually dead men and women existing in this world. Paul then goes on to explain that the new birth gives believers life. Ephesians 2:4–5; "But God is so rich in mercy, and he loved us so much, that even though we were dead because of our sins, he gave us life when he raised Christ from the dead."

I remember this personal impartation of life so vividly.

The world now looks very different to me since those early private moments of crying out to God to save me from my sinful living. He removed the film that had covered my life. He gave me a clarity to my existence that I had never known.

I later came to understand why I felt different. This is the most straightforward way I know to describe what happened: I had been moving through my life with a weight tied to one of my ankles. That heavy weight represented my sin, guilt, and shame. The heaviness only increased my sinfulness. The very things I hated—the behaviors and attitudes to alleviate the pain inside—only pushed me toward greater sin.

None of my religious activities could stop the downward spiral.

Because of our inherited sinful nature from our first parents, Adam and Eve, we are born with an inclination to please ourselves and to be our own gods. Our rebellion sets us at odds with Christ. Romans 5:10; "For if, while we were God's enemies, we were reconciled to him through the death of his Son, how much more, having been reconciled, shall we be saved through his life!" (NIV)

Scripture is clear—we cannot be reconciled with God due to our sinful state. We cannot have peace with God no matter how hard we try. Our best efforts are nothing but filthy rags. Isaiah 64:6 says, "We are all infected and impure with sin. When we display our righteous deeds, they are nothing but filthy rags. Like autumn leaves, we wither and fall, and our sins sweep us away like the wind."

Let me clarify: my life was still a mess, even after my new life began. There were still consequences to face. But I knew, with everything within me I had received a new start. Just as I had received Selah Kate's fresh, new life into my hands, God had received my new spiritual life into his. I had been birthed into his kingdom.

I was like a wide-eyed little girl exploring a beautiful new world. Because of the transformation that took place within me, the twenty-one days spent in the hospital after my accident remain one of the greatest treasures of my life.

To pursue the greatest commandment of loving God with all our capability and to love his people, we must first know God. We cannot know him if we are not connected to him.

We find Nicodemus again in John 7:50–52: "Then Nicodemus, the leader who had met with Jesus earlier, spoke up: 'Is it legal to convict a man before he is given a hearing?' he asked. They replied, 'Are you from Galilee, too? Search the Scriptures and see for yourself—no prophet ever comes from Galilee!'"

Though Nicodemus is not directly defending Christ, he is contending for justice on his behalf.

His final appearance is in John 19:38–40. "Afterward, Joseph of Arimathea, who had been a secret disciple of

Jesus (because he feared the Jewish leaders), asked Pilate for permission to take down Jesus's body. When Pilate gave permission, Joseph came and took the body away. With him came Nicodemus, the man who had come to Jesus at night. He brought about seventy-five pounds of perfumed ointment made from myrrh and aloes. Following Jewish burial custom, they wrapped Jesus's body with the spices in long sheets of linen cloth."

This portion of Scripture leads me to consider that Nicodemus had entered the kingdom. He had been born from above. With boldness, Nicodemus laid aside his reputation in an extravagant, tender, and intimate display of affection for Jesus.

CHAPTER EIGHT:
A NEW KIND OF LIFE

> In Him was life, and that life was the light of all mankind. (John 1:4)

If you've followed Christ for any length of time, you've likely lost connection with the wonder of your new birth. As humans, we lose appreciation for unique moments and personal treasures as time unfolds.

For believers, keeping the dynamics of the second birth in view generates vitality for living, and provides an ongoing source of passion for Christ.

The new birth, also known as regeneration, is supernatural. The most miraculous event in life, our rebirth comes directly from God. Like a baby being born, we are birthed into God's family. We find this truth in Romans 8:16–17: "For his Spirit joins with our spirit to affirm that we are God's children. And since we are his children, we are his heirs."

We were born into this world to be reborn spiritually. Our standing as a son or daughter of our Lord secures our identity. Here we discover our purpose. We must never minimize the value of our lives and purpose.

Scripture verifies the changeless reality that the entire human race is born spiritually dead to Christ. Until the evening of May 21, 1990, I had existence but did not have eternal life—the kind of life Jesus came to give.

I know, without any uncertainty, if I had died in my car accident, I would have stepped into an eternity of death and hell. This understanding is not according to a critique, personal or otherwise, but according to the Word of God. I did not possess eternal life. Romans 6:23 tells us, "For the wages of sin is death, but the gift of God is eternal life in Christ Jesus our Lord." (NIV)

I knew about God but did not have eternal life in Christ. Head knowledge does not generate the new birth.

The New Testament is abundantly clear; Jesus came to bring a different kind of life. John 3:16 presents this truth: "For this is how God loved the world: He gave his one and only Son so that everyone who believes in him will not perish but have eternal life."

Through our second birth, we gain access to this life. John 10:10: "The thief comes only to steal and kill and destroy; I have come that they may have life, and have it to the full." (NIV)

The Greek word translated "life" in John 10:10 is "zoe." This is the life of God imparted into our dead spirits. First John 5:11–12 says, "And this is what God has testified: He has given us eternal life, and this life is in his Son. Whoever has the Son has life; whoever does not have God's Son does not have life."

The new birth is Christ in you. God brings forth life where there was once death. Union with Jesus is everything.

In my early years with Christ, I read a book by C. S. Lewis titled *Mere Christianity*. An excerpt from his book captures this dramatic exchange of death for life.

> When we come to man, the highest of the animals, we get the completest resemblance to God which we know of. (There may be creatures in other worlds who are more

> like God than man is, but we do not know about them.) Man not only lives but loves and reasons: biological life reaches its highest known level in him.
>
> But what man, in his natural condition, has not got, does not have, is spiritual life—the higher and different sort of life that exists in God.[1]

Lewis continues to contrast biological life and zoe, or eternal life, using the image of statues. "A man who changed from having *bios* to having zoe would have gone through as big a change as a statue, which changed from being a carved stone to being a real man."[2]

Our parents gave us biological life—a physical life that gave us existence, but is also decomposing or winding down. When born from above, we are introduced into a life that never decays and only gets better as we age.

Sometimes, the miracle work of Christ's gift of eternal life works gently. Other times, it rushes in dramatically. One way is no greater than the other.

I think of the apostle Paul in Acts chapter 9 and his distinct conversion. I can connect with his experience. In my story, the surge of divine life was intense. However eternal life comes, we are new and changed. First Corinthians 5:17 explains, "This means that anyone who belongs to Christ has become a new person. The old life is gone; a new life has begun!"

This new life is not superficial, taking root at the core of our being. Through the power of the Holy Spirit, Christ gives us a new heart equipped with new affections and attitudes. He provides us with a will turned toward God.

Jesus tells us in John 14:6 "I am the way, the truth, and the life. No one can come to the Father except through me." The life Jesus gives is the only true life that exists. Salvation only comes through Christ, not Jesus plus something else. Christ is all we need.

New life is not turning over a new leaf or behavior modification. These things come with time. As we grow and develop spiritually, we become like "A good tree [that] produces good fruit" (Matthew 7:17).

As I shared, my conversion was dramatic. Overwhelmed by the strength of my love for God, I began to read the Bible with intensity. I learned later this was part of God's plan for our new birth as Paul explains in Romans 5:5: "And this hope will not lead to disappointment. For we know how dearly God loves us, because he has given us the Holy Spirit to fill our hearts with his love."

Every detail in my world shifted as I learned about Christ through the Scriptures. They gave way to new affections, new understanding, and a peace I had never experienced.

CHAPTER NINE:
LEGACY

> But I lavish unfailing love for a thousand generations on those who love me and obey my commands.
> (Deuteronomy 5:10)

Through a series of unusual events and God's providential care, I find myself writing this chapter in the home of my daughter-in-law's grandparents. Her grandparents have long since left the earth and gone home to Jesus. My husband and I are surrounded by shelves filled with books and teachings about God in every room. The walls are crowded with Scriptures and quotes of the promises of Christ.

Theirs is a legacy of two lives dedicated to the glory of our Lord.

The idea of legacy has intrigued me since the night I was born again and remains at the core of my life.

Three short sentences have been my traveling companions throughout the last thirty-plus years. I honestly can't recall if they came from within me or if they are words I read or heard spoken. These words have guided me throughout my journey with Christ.

I have received a legacy. I am living out a legacy. One day, I will pass on a legacy.

Merriam-Webster's defines "legacy" as something a predecessor hands down.

An excellent visual of this definition is the relay race. I was never a great athlete, but some of the insight I gained from my middle school coach, who taught us how to run the four-hundred-meter relay, has remained with me over the years.

He explained we must correctly pass the baton to win the race. Most of our success was based on how well we transferred the small cylinder from runner to runner. The runner had to hold it in the right hand and grip firmly near the base. We were to face forward and not continually look back. When we felt the baton slapped into our hands, we were to run with everything we had and then pass the baton to the next runner.

Our legacy is the baton. I received a legacy, am creating one, and am passing one on. Our life story is the race we are running—the space of time in which our legacy is created.

Hebrews 12:1–3 is a powerful example of running our race in Scripture:

> Therefore, since we are surrounded by such a huge crowd of witnesses to the life of faith, let us strip off every weight that slows us down, especially the sin that so easily trips us up. And let us run with endurance the race God has set before us. We do this by keeping our eyes on Jesus, the champion who initiates and perfects our faith. Because of the joy awaiting him, he endured the cross, disregarding its shame. Now he is seated in the place of honor beside God's throne. Think of all the hostility he endured from sinful people; then you won't become weary and give up.

Race is an athletic term that would have been well understood by the culture of that time and is still well understood today. The contest begins at a starting point and ends at a finish line. When we translate this idea into the spiritual realm, the starting point is the moment we step into our new life as followers of Jesus. When we step out of the kingdom of darkness and place our foot into the kingdom of Christ.

The finish line occurs when our eyes close in earthly death and we open them to look into the face of Jesus.

The time between our starting point and our finish line—our life story in Christ—is the race we run.

I am stirred deep in my soul when I read these opening verses in Hebrews 12. The words prompt me to recall vividly when I heard the starting gun go off.

A friend took a picture of me within the first few days of my hospital stay. When I view this photo, I immediately see beyond my physical brokenness. I remain aware of what was happening inside the young woman looking back at me.

That picture of me, with all my broken bones and other complications, didn't look like I was ready to run my race. I don't look capable of ever running any race.

When we think of a race or an athletic event, whether we're competing or not, we know the athlete will work hard to be in great shape, often the best form of their life. But throughout the Scripture, we hear again and again we all start our race broken.

Ephesians 2:1–3 says, "Once you were dead because of your disobedience and your many sins. You used to live in sin, just like the rest of the world, obeying the devil—the commander of the powers in the unseen world. He is the spirit at work in the hearts of those who refuse to obey God. All of us used to live that way."

When I began my race, I wasn't just physically broken. I was in the middle of a divorce. I was living with the results of the poor choices in my past and the generational baggage I had acquired. I was bumping up against all kinds of devastating darkness.

I was in the worst shape of my life—physically, spiritually, and emotionally.

For years, I had been bound and enslaved by the enemy's darkness. But when Christ took me out of darkness, and I stepped into the light of his kingdom, for the first time, I was aware I was in a race.

First Peter 2:9 explains what I experienced: "But you are a chosen people, a royal priesthood, a holy nation, God's special possession, that you may declare the praises of him who called you out of darkness into his wonderful light." (NIV)

For the first time ever, I felt the desire, the energy, and the hope to step off the starting block. I felt free to run. I wanted to run and had a goal to start running toward!

First Corinthians 9:24–27 explains this: "Don't you realize that in a race everyone runs, but only one person gets the prize? So run to win! All athletes are disciplined in their training. They do it to win a prize that will fade away, but we do it for an eternal prize. So I run with purpose in every step, I am not just shadow boxing. I discipline my body like an athlete, training it to do what it should. Otherwise, I fear that after preaching to others I myself might be disqualified."

The apostle Paul is cheering us on, and I believe he was encouraging himself too.

Hebrews 12:1 tells us that God has set a specific race in front of each of us. Paul is encouraging us to run our race to win. We need to run with purpose and intention in every step we take.

At the end of Paul's life, he is satisfied with the race he ran. He tells us in 2 Timothy 4:7: "I have fought the good fight, I have finished the race, and I have remained faithful."

Throughout Paul's life journey in Christ, he ran to win. He completed his race with purpose and intention, his legacy building with every step. At all times, Paul kept his target in view. He kept his eye on the finish line.

As I pursue the finish line and God's ultimate purpose for my life, creating my legacy with every stride, I can hear the Spirit of God whisper his promise. "But I lavish unfailing love for a thousand generations on those who love me and obey my commands" (Deuteronomy 5:10).

The car accident got my attention. I knew my life and priorities needed to change. I knew the legacy taking shape was not the one I wanted to leave behind.

In Mark 12:30–31, Jesus gives us a twofold approach to life: love God and love people. These weren't just words. Christ lived out this command perfectly as he ran his race—his life story here on earth.

His legacy has had a more significant impact than any other individual in the history of the world. The Son of Man left a legacy of loving God perfectly and loving people sacrificially. Jesus, fully God and fully man, loved God completely—with every aspect of his humanity.

When Christ offers us his plan of salvation, he provides an opportunity to change our heritage. As I lived out the twenty-one days in the hospital, one question invaded my thoughts. What if my story had ended here?

Our life story is the race we are running—the space of time in which our legacy is created. I shudder to think of the legacy I would have placed in the hands of my two young sons had my story ended in that hospital.

Mercifully, my legacy has grown over the last thirty-four years to embrace six adult children (Plus three daughters-in-law and one son-in-law) and fourteen grandchildren. As my legacy is formed by each choice to love God above all else, I am creating a solid ground where my children and grandchildren can run.

Like you, my story is interspersed with difficulties. The challenges can become overwhelming. But I keep my running shoes on with the help of words from Scripture, as those written in 3 John 1:4: "I could have no greater joy than to hear that my children (*and grandchildren*) are following the truth" (emphasis added).

CHAPTER TEN: THE DEVELOPMENT OF ENDURANCE

> And let us run with endurance the race God has set before us.
> (Hebrews 12:1)

We've determined the distinct boundaries of our race: the starting point and the finish line. We've concluded God is the one who laid the course before us, and we see in Hebrews 12:1 we are to run our race with endurance.

Endurance, a familiar term in the athletic arena, refers to "the ability to do something difficult or stressful for an extended period."[1] It involves resisting the urge to surrender and refusing to collapse under challenging circumstances or trials. In other words, endurance is about maintaining a steady pace.

Our race is a marathon, not a fifty-yard dash. The athlete must be in prime condition to compete in this strenuous long-distance race. The competitor's preparation is not solely focused on the physical aspect of the race. To finish well, the serious contender must begin with an accurate mindset, knowing the race will be long and difficult.

At the starting point of our life journey in Christ, we're fresh and full of determination and enthusiasm. We have the mindset to do whatever is necessary to live well and cross the finish line. However, at some point, we will inevitably experience fatigue.

When athletes run a fifty-yard dash, they push off from the starting block with a surge of power and energy, knowing the race will be complete in a few seconds. However, marathon runners need to adopt the mindset that their race will take a measured amount of time. Embracing this knowledge will help them endure, persevere, and reach the finish line.

How do we develop endurance?

Romans 5:3–4 tells us, "We can rejoice, too, when we run into problems and trials, for we know that they help us develop endurance. And endurance develops strength of character, and character strengthens our confident hope of salvation."

James 1:2–4 continues with the same thought, "Dear brothers and sisters, when troubles of any kind come your way, consider it an opportunity for great joy. For you know that when your faith is tested, your endurance has a chance to grow. So let it grow, for when your endurance is fully developed, you will be perfect and complete, needing nothing."

Both portions of Scripture reveal a shocking concept. Romans 5:3 tells us to rejoice in our trials, and James 1:2 tells us to embrace our trials as an opportunity for great joy.

What a challenging concept to grasp. This is another new aspect of life in the kingdom of God.

The Bible gives abundant testimony; even as believers, we will encounter trials. No one is exempt. There's no escape. Peter goes so far as to tell us in 1 Peter 4:12 not to be surprised or think it strange when we encounter problems. Our life story is a succession of experiences—both good and challenging—along with trials and burdens.

We put our running shoes on and hear the explosive sound of the starting gun. We begin the race with the finish line in view. Jesus reminds us there will be hurdles to overcome between our starting point and the finish line. He encourages us to choose joy when facing them.

You've got to be kidding, right? First, God tells me I will face trials, and then he tells me to choose joy amid them.

When I first came to know Jesus, those around me told me life would be easier. There would be fewer struggles. This was great news for a newly single mom with two little boys. But as I began to study his Word for myself and experience life in the kingdom, I found their assurance to be untrue.

Over time, James 1:2–4 has become a lifeline for me, a new perspective and filter to process my pain, sorrow, and trials. I believe a new perspective is what Jesus intends for all of us. Choosing joy in the face of hardships and difficulties is not a natural human response. As believers, we must make a conscious effort to face our trials with joy and perseverance. According to Scripture, our struggles are designed to mature our faith in Christ.

Trials, the places in our lives where our comfort and peace are disrupted, are intended to strengthen us. We are given the choice to obey God and remain confident in his care and provision or disobey God and doubt him.

Philippians 3:1 admonishes, "Whatever happens, my dear brothers and sisters, rejoice in the Lord. I never get tired of telling you these things, and I do it to safeguard your faith."

Here, Paul encourages us to choose the same mindset Jesus chose—to rejoice in the Lord at all times. If we have the mindset of Christ, we will believe whatever God places in our lives is for our best.

The radical idea of choosing joy in the middle of our trials does not mean we deny our emotional pain. Jesus isn't telling us to slap on our happy face and deny we are hurting. Powerful emotions are real and unavoidable when we experience difficult and hurtful moments. Still, we can walk in joy.

One of the best definitions of joy I found is from a book called *Choose Joy Because Happiness Isn't Enough* by Kay Warren: "Joy is the settled assurance that God is in control of all the details of my life, the quiet confidence that ultimately everything is going to be all right, and the determined choice to praise God in all things."[2]

Warren goes on to clarify that the details of our lives include car accidents, cancer, financial problems, miscarriage, depression, and every other trial we may face.

Romans 8:28 confirms this: "And we know that God causes everything to work together for the good of those who love God and are called according to his purpose for them."

Each of us will experience loss. We will all mourn at some point in our lives. Everyone struggles with difficulties—they are unavoidable. But for those who follow Jesus, we know our pain and trials are never wasted.

Six years into my journey with Christ, my family experienced a difficult season of loss. One of those losses was the death of my sixteen-year-old stepson, Trevor.

Trevor shared our home for four years before May 27, 1996. On his way home from work that evening, Trevor was killed in a car accident.

This day is marked for me by several vivid details. With no cell phones at the time, Trevor would call before leaving work so we could watch for him in case of car trouble. When he didn't arrive home, we left our two youngest sons in the care of their older brother, who had just returned home from college, and went looking for him, assuming Trevor had some type of car problem.

My husband and I came upon the wreck shortly after the accident occurred. The local police department was already on the scene. I can still picture Trevor's Nike tennis shoes pointing down on the asphalt.

I cringe when I recall the deep grief on the faces of my husband and stepdaughter when she joined us at the site of the accident. I remember the dread I felt at the painful experience of telling our other three sons their brother had died.

In this dark place, I first experienced the joy spoken of in the Scriptures. As the days unfolded and we grieved as a family, there was this place deep within me that stayed anchored in the hope of the gospel.

The joy Jesus offered me through my relationship with him penetrated every part of me. The truth of the gospel brought me comfort and strengthened me as I cared for both myself and my family during this difficult and sorrowful time.

In his book *Cultivating a Life of Worship and Joy*, Dallas Willard explains joy this way: "Joy is not about pleasure, a mere sensation, but a pervasive and constant sense of well-being. Hope in the goodness of God is joy's indispensable support."[3]

Willard's description of joy opened my mind to comprehend the quality of joy. As I reflect on the past and my journey with Christ through the dark places of sorrow and hurt, I recall vividly that pervasive sense of well-being. I remember a profound sense of knowing God saw me and was with me. I found strength in knowing God was in control of my life and his intentions towards me were good.

Our understanding of joy is crucial. If our knowledge is inadequate, we will equate joy with happiness. Happiness is an emotion that changes with our circumstances. Joy isn't tied to our circumstances nor dependent on how we feel.

As followers of Jesus, the source of our joy is hope and trust in God.

In Scripture, the word endurance is consistently linked to the quality of hope. "For everything that was written in the past was written to teach us, so that through the endurance taught in the Scriptures and the encouragement they provide, we might have hope" (Romans 15:4 NIV).

In Romans 5:3–4 and James 1:2–4, the writers also reveal an uncomfortable but beautiful revelation. The places in life we want to avoid or quickly vacate help us develop endurance. These difficulties produce great spiritual benefits.

For the endurance athlete, half the joy comes from finishing the race and evaluating their time. The other half comes from pushing through the pain, discomfort, and a persistent desire to quit.

Processing our pain and trials through the words of Scripture gives us a fresh outlook. When we fully understand this—when we are determined to choose joy no matter what comes—we gain a new perspective with which to run our race.

CHAPTER ELEVEN: THE NECESSITY OF ENDURANCE

> Patient endurance is what you need now so that you will continue to do God's will. Then you will receive all that he has promised.
> (Hebrews 10:36)

We've examined what spiritual stamina is and how endurance is developed. But why is it necessary for our lives?

Perseverance is necessary for spiritual growth and maturity. Romans 5:4 tells us, "And endurance develops strength of character, and character strengthens our confident hope of salvation."

Not only do we gain spiritual maturity, but the race—our life journey in Christ—becomes a testimony to those around us who don't know Jesus. We make Jesus known to the world through our steadfastness.

We demonstrate our faith is real and solid when we persevere instead of wavering. Faith testifies to those around us that we put our trust in what God has done in our past, what he is doing in our present, and we trust him with our future.

We let a dying world know Jesus is alive.

Patience is required to finish our race. Endurance is necessary to complete the unique and specific destiny God has laid out before us. Hebrews 10:36 clarifies this need, "Patient endurance is what you need now so that you will continue to do God's will. Then you will receive all that he has promised."

We identified perseverance, how it gives rise to strength, and the purpose it plays in our lives. But what is the birthplace of endurance? Scripture provides the answer. Second Thessalonians 3:5 tells us, "May the Lord lead your hearts into a full understanding and expression of the love of God and *the patient endurance that comes from Christ*" (emphasis added).

Christ has gone before us and has already run the race. He endured the cross and reached the finish line. Through his death, resurrection, and ascension, we have acquired access to supernatural perseverance through his victory.

Because of Christ's accomplishment, we have gained entrance into God's promises. Hebrews 4:16 explains this for us: "So let us come boldly to the throne of our gracious God. There we will receive his mercy, and we will find grace to help us when we need it most."

We need endurance on the way to the promises of God.

We must realize the enemy's mission is to stop us. He wants to discourage us and lead us to a place of deep weariness; he is eager for us to step out of our race. The devil desires us to lose sight of the people we are called to impact and influence for the kingdom of God.

In those complex spaces in our lives—the losses we experience through death, marital difficulties, parenting challenges, divorce, and illness—the enemy wants to exhaust us, so we will quit and give up on God.

Satan's goal is to stop you in your tracks and rob you of your legacy in Christ.

We find renewal in Scripture. Galatians 6:9 encourages us to keep going and directs us to the need for steadfastness:

"Let us not become weary in doing good, for at the proper time we will reap a harvest if we do not give up" (NIV).

The words "perseverance" and "endurance" are used interchangeably in various Bible translations. Some translations will also use the words "patience" or "long-suffering." These words are synonyms or phrases with the same or nearly identical meanings, all conveying the idea of duration.

However, Greek, the original language of the New Testament, uses two main words for endurance in Greek.

The first is "hupomone," defined as "holding fast while being patient and not surrendering to trials." The second is "makrothumia," which means "to be long-suffering—keeping a patient and forgiving attitude toward people rather than trials." This clarification has helped me understand the enemy's tactics at a deeper level.

Romans 5:4 explains that forbearance develops strength of character. In terms of character, patient continuance is not only having the capability to stay strong when life is difficult but also having the humility to stay forgiving and loving to avoid becoming rigid and bitter. With the Spirit's aid, we can remain steadfast and strong and be tenderhearted. This is the character perseverance generates.

No life portrays this character more than the life of Christ.

This is why Hebrews 12:1, 2 tells us to keep our eyes on Jesus; "And let us run with endurance the race God has set before us. We do this by keeping our eyes on Jesus, the champion who initiates and perfects our faith. Because of the joy awaiting him, he *endured* the cross, disregarding its shame" (emphasis added).

As we read about Jesus's life in the four Gospels, we can observe where he demonstrated steadfastness, where he exhibited endurance in difficult situations, resisted surrender, and refused to collapse under challenging circumstances. Our Lord remained loving and forgiving in the harshest of conditions.

When dealing with people and their personalities, trials, and grueling settings, Jesus remained patient under stressful conditions. He kept his mind strong and focused by clinging to the truth. Even when situations didn't appear to make sense in his immediate circumstances, Christ held on to the promises of his Father.

Jesus remained strong. He was looking past the cross, past the pain, and past his death. He kept his eyes fixed on the finish line and the joy that lay before him.

In the places of deepest hurt and pain, Christ kept his heart tender and loving. At the point of most significant physical, emotional, and spiritual pain—at the peak of horrible violence—we hear Jesus asking God to forgive those who were torturing him.

Through all that, Christ endured, he kept his course; he stayed in his race. He pushed forward and continued to make progress. Jesus kept his joy.

God can take our most difficult circumstances and transform us into people with a greater ability for love, but endurance is necessary.

We can boldly approach our gracious and patient God and ask for the perseverance that comes from his son, Jesus Christ. In our places of harshest circumstances and deepest hurts, we can fix our eyes on Jesus and model his example. We won't do it perfectly, but if our focus is on Christ, we will run the race well.

CHAPTER TWELVE:
RUNNING TO WIN

> Don't you realize that in a race, everyone runs, but only one person gets the prize? So run to win!
> (1 Corinthians 9:24)

The apostle Paul frequently speaks of "running the race" throughout the New Testament. Paul's words carry the implications of a physical event, but he reveals how believers should spiritually live.

We may wonder why Paul, as an Orthodox Jew and Pharisee, likened the analogy of a Christ follower to that of an athlete. Sporting events were not part of the Jewish culture. However, one of the stadiums most essential to Paul's knowledge would have been in Athens, Greece. Athens was a place of idols, gods, and competitions. Acts 17:16 informs us, "While Paul was waiting for them in Athens, he was deeply troubled by all the idols he saw everywhere in the city." At the time, there were approximately ten thousand people in Athens. The city was estimated to have had approximately thirty thousand statues of gods. Athens was known for having more gods than people.

Competitions were held every four years in honor of the goddess Athena. The games consisted of layers of events. The first was a religious festival where idol worshipers made sacrifices to Athena, the protector of the city. This celebration was followed by a cultural event that included poetic and musical competitions. Exhibitions were held in athletic and equestrian events. Some of the athletic competitions were wrestling, boxing, and running competitions.

Paul was also aware of the culture of Corinth, where games were held every two years to celebrate the Greek god Poseidon. Acts 18:1 tells us Paul left Athens and went to Corinth. He remained there for a year and a half. Paul's athletic imagery displays his ability to communicate in the language and ideas familiar to his audience. Like Christ, Paul used practical applications from the culture and everyday lives of his audience.

In 1 Corinthians 9:24–27, Paul admonishes, "Don't you realize that in a race everyone runs, but only one person gets the prize? So run to win! All athletes are disciplined in their training. They do it to win a prize that will fade away, but we do it for an eternal prize. So I run with purpose in every step. I am not just shadowboxing. I discipline my body like an athlete, training it to do what it should. Otherwise, I fear that after preaching to others, I myself might be disqualified."

Paul not only compares our lives to an athletic event, he also emphasizes that *how* we compete is a serious matter. In verse 24, Paul instructs us to compete to win. The very nature of how we pursue the prize is significant.

Today, in our Olympic Games, the winning athletes are awarded gold, silver, and bronze medals. In ancient times, there were no second- or third-place awards. Winning was everything.

In Philippians 3:12–14, Paul sets an example for us to follow: "Not that I have already obtained all this, or have already arrived at my goal, but I press on to take hold of that for which Christ Jesus took hold of me. Brothers and sisters, I do not consider myself yet to have taken hold of it. But one thing I do: forgetting what is behind and straining toward what is ahead, I press on toward the goal to win the prize for which God has called me heavenward in Christ Jesus" (NIV).

A few verses later, in Philippians 3:17, he instructs us to "pattern your lives after mine."

Paul's letter coaches us in the art of living well. He presents to us the skill of how to escape a life of emptiness and meaningless moments. He reveals how to make every moment count. The apostle's words create a picture of an alert and clear-minded competitor, someone attentive to his life. He is fully present and self-aware. Paul is intentional and aggressive with every step of his race. Paul modeled what genuine living looks like in the kingdom of God.

Jesus tells us in John 10:10, "The thief's purpose is to steal and kill and destroy. My purpose is to give them a rich and satisfying life." How we engage with our journey in Christ is a factor that determines our level of life satisfaction.

As followers of Jesus, we often approach our race with a passive attitude. This casual approach was a foreign concept to the apostle Paul. If we accept Paul's invitation to pattern our lives after him, we will experience a rich and deep satisfaction at the core of our lives as we passionately pursue the finish line.

How we participate in the course God has set before us is the practical application—the working out—of Mark 12:30, to love God with all our heart, soul, mind, and strength. Our zeal and vitality for life increase as our love for God grows. This passionate love for God fuels our desire to love others, pursue the finish line, and win the prize.

The hope—and command—of the gospel is we engage in life with all our human capacity and love God and others well.

In Hebrews 12, we are told to fix our eyes on Jesus. Christ instructs us to run the way he ran.

He did not run his race, so we wouldn't have to. He didn't save us, so we could sit on the sidelines and observe. We were created to participate—to pursue the prize.

We were made to run!

Scripture directs us to live as intended—to glorify the Father. First Corinthians 10:31 teaches us, "So whether you eat or drink, or whatever you do, do it all for the glory of God."

We bring honor and praise to God through the very nature of how we contend for the finish line.

In Philippians 3, Paul clarifies he has not obtained the prize. He understood perfection would not be achieved in this world. Becoming Christlike is not a single moment of achievement; it is a lifelong process of growth—a goal we pursue until we see Jesus face-to-face. Perfection only comes when we stand in the presence of our King.

A progression or maturing occurs within our lives as we encounter obstacles. Deep in the space between our trials and the strengthening of our endurance, we become more like Christ.

Our call is to run the best we can in each segment of our lives and to give our all to God. Verse 12 also reveals Paul's passionate priority in life: "I press on to take hold of that for which Christ Jesus took hold of me" (NIV).

From Paul's encounter with Christ on the Damascus road until he went home to Jesus, Paul took the course set before him seriously and ran with enthusiasm.

For Paul, taking hold of Christ was a personal and passionate pursuit. Becoming like Jesus was the greatest obsession of his life. He left no question as to where he placed his devotion.

How we compete demonstrates who we are, pointing others in the direction of our true passions. Our pursuit reveals who we trust, to whom we are devoted, and what we believe.

As a follower of Christ, when I run to win, I am demonstrating to those around me that Christ lives within me (Galatians 2:20).

CHAPTER THIRTEEN: THE HEAVENLY PRIZE

> I press on to reach the end of the race and receive the heavenly prize for which God, through Christ Jesus, is calling us.
> (Philippians 3:14)

The apostle Paul focuses on a well-defined objective in Philippians 3: the heavenly prize. Reaching the goal involves an intimate journey with Christ, which draws us toward spiritual maturity. Paul, often regarded as the greatest apostle, vulnerably shares his journey of transformation. His intensity toward becoming Christlike is evident. At a designated time, each believer will cross the finish line and win the prize of meeting Jesus in eternity.

Second Peter 3:18 identifies how to progress toward the finish line: "But grow in the grace and knowledge of our Lord and Savior, Jesus Christ" (NIV).

When we are born again, God begins shaping us into the image of his Son, and he is faithful to complete what he began. We find this promise in Philippians 1:6: "And I am certain that God, who began the good work within you, will continue his work until it is finally finished on the day when Christ Jesus returns."

Mark 12:30 verifies we are to pursue spiritual maturity wholeheartedly. "And you must love the Lord your God with all your heart, all your soul, all your mind, and all your strength."

Like the apostle Paul, we must understand and believe we hold the world's most essential and valuable possession. In Philippians 3:10, Paul tells us he wants to know Christ and experience the mighty power of his resurrection.

Each of us should consider: "Does my relationship with Jesus reflect enthusiasm and intimacy? Am I so passionate about my relationship with Christ that I want to share his message with the world? Or do I give the impression my Christianity is dull and trivial?

The pursuit of Christlikeness dominated every sphere of Paul's life. Jesus instructs us in Matthew 6:33: "Seek the Kingdom of God above all else, and live righteously, and he will give you everything you need." *Everything* includes our families, marriages, careers, financial needs, and all other necessities of life. We must pursue Christlikeness. As we make Jesus our single focus and become like him, the Holy Spirit helps us navigate the other details of our lives.

In Philippians 3, Paul publicly and transparently evaluates his Christian journey. He gives an honest and accurate account of his spiritual life. The apostle Paul developed a healthy sense of self-awareness. The tone of his writing communicates Paul was not hesitant but eager to examine himself. He did not ignore the characteristics that were not hitting the mark. He worked to develop the aspects of his personality that needed to be perfected, matured, and more like Christ.

Paul embraced this knowledge and looked toward the future. He moved forward with the understanding that becoming like Christ is a process.

If we are not careful, we can come to a standstill in our pursuit of growth following our salvation experience. We can become complacent in our walk with Jesus. Merely escaping hell is not life's goal. Paul, this great apostle, shows us we are never finished; there is always more.

Many observers would agree Paul was the most extraordinary Christian ever to live. Yet even though he wrote thirteen New Testament books, he remained dissatisfied with his progress. He was still striving to reach the goal of becoming like Christ.

In verse 12, Paul tells us: "I don't mean to say that I have already achieved these things or have already achieved perfection." Paul knew Christ, but he wanted more.

Paul had been a believer for approximately twenty-five years at this point in his life. This great man of God conveys to us he understood he was still a work in progress. Although he was a Christian leader, the apostle Paul remained teachable, a quality essential for transformation.

Like Paul, as I reflect on my life, a few questions bring my journey into focus:

- Am I still eager to learn about God and his kingdom?
- Do I continue to desire to learn and be taught from God's Word?

The answer is reflected in the time I spend with God. This comes in many forms, including worship, personal devotions, attending church, and engaging in Bible study.

In the latter portion of verse 13, Paul tells us: "But one thing I do: forgetting what is behind and straining toward what is ahead" (NIV). He is straining toward the future.

The word "straining" creates a mental picture of a runner with his chest thrown out and reaching forward to overtake the finish line. Paul was giving the race all he had. There was an intense energy behind Paul's determination to reach the finish line.

In the same sentence, he tells us to forget our past. If we examine the details of Paul's testimony throughout

Scripture, we see he has not erased the memory of his past. The word "forgetting" in this passage means refusing to focus on. Paul refused to let his past successes inflate his pride, and he did not allow his past sinfulness to define his self-worth. He continued to grow into his new identity (2 Corinthians 5:17).

I believe Paul's intense energy and his ability to strain toward the future were generated because he kept his testimony at the forefront of his mind.

Right before Paul's encounter with Jesus on the Damascus road, we read in Acts 9:1–2: "Meanwhile, Saul [also known as Paul, Acts 13:9] was uttering threats with every breath and was eager to kill the Lord's followers. So he went to the high priest. He requested letters addressed to the synagogues in Damascus, asking for their cooperation in arresting any followers of the Way he found there. He wanted to bring them—both men and women—back to Jerusalem in chains."

Paul lived within the tension of his past and future. With intentionality, he recalled the grace of God on his life, using his testimony as a necessary companion to fuel his race. In verse 14, Paul tells us, "I press on." He is running the race with an all-out human effort.

The Christian race is a challenging, lifelong process. To run a good race takes discipline and dedication. However, we will experience our greatest contentment in life as we strive to become more like Christ.

CHAPTER FOURTEEN:
THE GIFT OF TIME

In the beginning, God created the heavens and the earth. (Genesis 1:1)

In Genesis 1:1, we read the very first words of the Bible: "In the beginning, God created the heavens and the earth.

"In the beginning" records the creation of time. "God created the heavens" marks the creation of space, "and the earth" indicates the creation of matter. Jesus, the creator of all things, is the author of science.

John 1:3 supports this reality. "God created everything through him *(Jesus)*, and nothing was created except through him" (emphasis added).

Time, space, and matter form a perfect continuum. They are inseparable. One cannot exist without the other. Time was created, and time had an absolute beginning.

A crucial fact we must consider is God existed before time began. Scripture verifies this truth in Psalm 90:2: "Before the mountains were born, before you gave birth to the earth and the world, from beginning to end, you are God."

Second Timothy 1:9 declares, "For God saved us and called us to live a holy life. He did this, not because we deserved it, but because that was his plan from before the beginning of time—to show us his grace through Christ Jesus."

Jude 25 gives reference to our timeline, directing us to our history on earth. "All glory to him who alone is God, our Savior through Jesus Christ our Lord. All glory, majesty, power, and authority are his before all time, and in the present, and beyond all time! Amen."

The Bible presents our time on earth as having a definite beginning, an end, and a God-given purpose. He had a plan for creation, and his plan will continue until completion. Paul clarified this in Ephesians 1:10: "And this is the plan: At the right time he will bring everything together under the authority of Christ—everything in heaven and on earth."

This Scripture communicates God has set a chronological set of events in motion. As Christians, we understand a biblical timeline has been unfolding since the fall of man.

Throughout the New Testament, we find evidence that Paul believed the return of Christ could happen in his generation. The anticipation of Christ's return provided the intense energy that drove Paul's life.

The apostle wrote in Romans 13:11: "This is all the more urgent, for you know how late it is; time is running out. Wake up, for our salvation is nearer now than when we first believed." This verse provides some apparent aspects of time. Not only did Paul indicate the approaching end of all time, but he also sharply focused on our personal timeline and place in history.

Most timelines representing biblical history begin with the fall of man. When Adam disobeyed God, he became subject to death. Romans 5:12 tells us, "When Adam sinned, sin entered the world. Adam's sin brought death, so death spread to everyone, for everyone sinned."

The moment Adam transgressed, he became vulnerable to the passage of time.

This knowledge is essential to our understanding that time is not only in sequence with space and matter—but due to Adam's sin—time is also in a continuum with sin and death. God created time, space, and matter, but until Adam sinned, he was not subject to or changed by it.

Even though we cannot fully comprehend the mystery of God knowing all things, we must recognize his primary intent. Our Father never desired we experience death, sin, and the breakdown of time.

In my research, time was repeatedly defined as "duration." Time is the duration during which something exists, and it is characterized or revealed by changes. Time and change go together. We observe time and change as our babies grow up, become teenagers, and leave home. We can see the effects of time as we compare past and present pictures of ourselves.

Time is necessary for change to occur. One of God's attributes is he is eternal. He exists in eternity, outside of time, and therefore remains unchanged. Hebrews 13:8 tells us God is the same yesterday, today, and forever.

Why is this essential for us to understand?

Our merciful God structured life so time becomes the place where Christ can redeem us. Our timeline and story become the place where Jesus can save us from sin and eternal death and transform our lives.

Understanding this truth gives profound relevance and undeniable value to our time. Our lives are more than just a birth certificate and a death certificate.

Christ's offer of redemption marks our timeline.

Galatians 4:4–5 encourages us this way, "But when the right time came, God sent his Son, born of a woman, subject to the law. God sent him to buy freedom for us who were slaves to the law so that he could adopt us as his very own children."

This is the purpose of every second, minute, hour, and day of our timeline.

Psalm 139 contains beautiful words and truths. Verse 5 is one of the most brilliant Scriptures regarding Jesus's movement in our life story.

Psalm 139:5: "You hem me in behind and before, and you lay your hand upon me" (NIV). This verse demonstrates Jesus's lovingkindness. The word hem provides us with a valuable word picture. To be hemmed in means I have borders; I have boundaries for protection.

Christ goes into my past and cares for me. Through my Savior's act of redemption, he has taken my past failures and sins and transformed them into something beautiful and valuable for his kingdom. Romans 8:28: "And we know that God causes everything to work together for the good of those who love God and are called according to his purpose for them."

The words "you lay your hand upon me" reveal if I have surrendered my life to Christ, he has entered my future to prepare the minutes, days, months, and years ahead of me.

As a wonderful Father, God's hand is on me and guides me into the future. He reaffirms the sense of comfort and security expressed by being hemmed in.

Psalm 139:15–16 exposes these limits: "You watched me as I was being formed in utter seclusion, as I was woven together in the dark of the womb. You saw me before I was born. Every day of my life was recorded in your book. Every moment was laid out before a single day had passed."

God directs and protects us within our timeline as we live out each twenty-four-hour day. He brings comfort and peace as we build our lives, knowing he controls everything.

Through Scripture, we know God is all-knowing, compassionate, and loving. He is a personal God. Luke 12:7 tells us he numbers the very hairs on our heads.

God's purpose in history is the creation of an all-encompassing community of people who love and honor

God with every dimension of their humanity—a Church that holds God at the very center of their lives.

This is the community envisioned in Mark 12:29–31: Jesus replied, "'And you must love the Lord your God with all your heart, all your soul, all your mind, and all your strength.' The second is equally important: 'Love your neighbor as yourself.' No other commandment is greater than these."

CHAPTER FIFTEEN: THE LIFE OF FAITH

> Abraham reasoned that if Isaac died, God was able to bring him back to life again.
> (Hebrews 11:19)

The Gospels—Matthew, Mark, Luke, and John—emphasize the humanity of Jesus. Being fully God and fully man, our Lord confined himself to time and space. Yet, if all we understand about Jesus comes from the Gospels, we will not have a complete picture of Christ.

The book of Hebrews is a remarkable segment of the New Testament, focusing on Jesus's life, death, and resurrection. The author is unknown, but we know the Scriptures were written under the inspiration of the Holy Spirit. The letter provides specific details providing a complete portrait of Christ and was delivered to a group of discouraged and frightened followers of Jesus. The author's intention is clear: to encourage believers to stand firm in their faith and not return to unbelief.

As Christianity spread in the first century, many new converts experienced hardship and persecution. Christians were beaten and thrown into prison. Their homes were raided, and some of the believers were tempted to abandon Christianity and return to their former Jewish traditions.

In chapter 11 of Hebrews, the writer takes the audience on a journey of remembrance, recalling those who had gone before them. The author presents a powerful and inspirational account of men and women who placed their faith in God's promises. The word "faith" appears twenty-seven times in this single chapter.

Faith is among the many religious terms we use when conversing with other believers. Some of us have grown up with this word, along with the implied understanding. But often, when confronted with the need to clarify our belief, we are limited in our explanation.

Faith is vital to our Christian journey and must be firmly established to pursue the greatest commandment with passion and effectiveness. Without great faith, we will run our race half-heartedly and cannot reach the heights to which God has called us.

As my life in the kingdom began to unfold, the message of faith was delivered to me as a leap into the unknown. My faith was equated to obedience. Don't get me wrong, I know there is an element of truth in both statements. However, as I studied the book of Hebrews, I encountered many aspects which challenged my initial understanding.

If faith is anything, it is a place where our eyes are opened to the knowledge of who Christ is and the facts surrounding the person of Jesus. As believers, our Savior is the object of our trust. Christ is where we direct and place our belief.

Scripture informs us biblical faith requires content. Romans 10:17 instructs, "So faith comes from hearing, that is, hearing the Good News about Christ." We can't trust what we don't know. Our ears receive the gospel, and our faith grows through the power of the Holy Spirit.

My spiritual rebirth on May 21, 1990, was a distinct moment in time and an immediate movement toward Jesus. As a new creation in Christ, my attitude and disposition changed. If we are authentically born again, the action of obedience toward God grows and gains strength over time.

Hebrews 11 records the conduct and choices of the great heroes of the faith. Biblical faith begins with thinking and results in obedient action.

While the author encourages us to imitate these great men and women, he also makes a solid point— they were ordinary people who lived lives of extreme faith. Moses, Sarah, Noah, and all the others were not superheroes.

We tend to put these great examples of faith on pedestals, keeping them out of reach of ordinary people like you and me. James 5:17 keeps them in a proper perspective: "Elijah was as human as we are, and yet when he prayed earnestly that no rain would fall, none fell for three and a half years!"

Hebrews 12 calls these testimonies to the life of faith "a huge crowd of witnesses." We are surrounded by a crowd of ordinary human beings who believed in God for great things. We can imitate them.

As I studied the account of Abraham and Sarah in Hebrews 11, two words were significant to my understanding of faith. The first is found in 11:11: "And by faith, even Sarah, who was past childbearing age, was enabled to bear children because she considered him faithful who had made the promise" (NIV).

Sarah (Abraham's wife) was about ninety years old when she received the promise from God she would have a baby. The word "considered" means to investigate, study, or think through a situation. Sarah considered whether the one making the promise was trustworthy.

She reasons they have been in the land God called them to, and God has provided for them completely. He has given them abundance and protection. She has experienced God's faithfulness. She concludes it is reasonable for her to believe God will do what he has promised.

Hebrews 11:17–19 details the story of Abraham: "It was by faith that Abraham offered Isaac as a sacrifice when God was testing him. Abraham, who had received God's promises, was ready to sacrifice his only son, Isaac, even though God had told him, 'Isaac is the son through whom your descendants will be counted.' Abraham reasoned that if Isaac died, God was able to bring him back to life again. And in a sense, Abraham did receive his son back from the dead."

The story of Abraham is based upon the assurance of a male heir. Everything God had promised Abraham hinged on a son. Many years later, when Abraham was well past the age of being able to have children physically, he received the promise.

Then God tells him to do something bizarre, to give up his promised son. What does Abraham do? Scripture tells us he reasoned.

The point of Abraham having a son—the reason Isaac existed—was because God had proven himself trustworthy. He had kept his promise. Abraham considered his relationship with God and determined it was logical for him to believe that however God chose to solve this problem, he would fulfill his promise.

Abraham had a choice, not just about his thoughts but also about his actions. The first thing he did was to think about God's faithfulness he had already experienced.

Building our lives on our belief in Christ is not unreasonable or irrational. He was a man whom Scripture confirms was fully God. He lived on the stage of history approximately two thousand years ago.

Hundreds of testimonies reflect on his life, death, and resurrection. In 1 Corinthians 15:3–8, the apostle Paul delivers an example: "I passed on to you what was most important and what had also been passed on to me. Christ died for our sins, just as the Scriptures said. He was buried, and he was raised from the dead on the third day, just as the Scriptures said. He was seen by Peter and then by the Twelve. After that, he was seen by more than 500 of his followers at one time, most of whom are still alive, though some have died. Then, he was seen by James and later by all the apostles. Last of all, as though I had been born at the wrong time, I also saw him."

Paul appeals to reason in his letter to Corinth. Jesus's life wasn't kept private or hidden. He lived his life at the center of history in one of the most prominent cities in the ancient world. Our faith rests on this reality. We can count on Jesus to fulfill the promises he has given us.

When we confidently embrace belief in Christ, our faith imparts passion and vision to pursue God in every area of our lives. This pursuit supplies us with the motivation to love others well.

CHAPTER SIXTEEN: THE PROMISE OF NO CONDEMNATION

> Therefore, there is now no condemnation for those who are in Christ Jesus.
> (Romans 8:1 NIV)

Our encounter with the gospel has the power to impact and transform our entire story. A new legacy is just one of the gifts we receive when we connect our lives to Jesus. This fresh legacy encompasses our past, present, and future.

Many of us come into the kingdom with heavy baggage. In places of brokenness, there are often dark shadows of shame and regret. This was my story. The guilt from my past held me hostage.

As I surrendered my life to Christ, I distinctly recall the moment I experienced God's forgiveness. In the divine exchange of death for life, I knew the shame had been removed from my story. Like an oversized, heavy coat, restricting my movements, the humiliation was finally gone. In Romans 8:1, the apostle Paul highlights this promise we receive at salvation: "Therefore, there is now no condemnation for those who are in Christ Jesus" (NIV).

At the moment of our new birth, we are positioned in Christ. Whenever Paul uses the phrase "in Christ," he refers to what Jesus accomplished through the cross, making new life in him possible.

In an article from the C. S. Lewis Institute, John Stott teaches, "The commonest description in the Scriptures of a follower of Jesus is that he or she is a person "in Christ." The expressions "in Christ," "in the Lord," and "in him" occur 164 times in the letters of Paul alone and are indispensable to an understanding of the New Testament. To be "in Christ" does not mean to be inside Christ, as tools are in a box or our clothes in a closet, but to be organically united to Christ, as a limb is in the body or a branch is in the tree. It is this personal relationship with Christ that is the distinctive mark of his authentic followers."[1]

The goal and work of faith is to place us in Christ. When we grasp the gospel, we know and understand the facts surrounding the message of salvation. We have put our trust and confidence in the person and work of Jesus.

The promise of "no condemnation" is specifically for the benefit of believers. God extends his promise to all who are in Christ. Being in Christ goes beyond attending church or belonging to a particular denomination. Those who have received Jesus as the Lord of their lives aren't condemned. This understanding gave me great comfort. My sinful past came with consequences I'd need to deal with and work through. But the shadow of guilt and shame could no longer prevent me from moving forward. Jesus had paid my penalty.

Romans 8:3–4 explains, "The law of Moses was unable to save us because of the weakness of our sinful nature. So God did what the law could not do. He sent his own Son in a body like the bodies we sinners have. And in that body, God declared an end to sin's control over us by giving his Son as a sacrifice for our sins. He did this so that the just requirement of the law would be fully satisfied for us, who no longer follow our sinful nature but instead follow the Spirit."

I can't be condemned because I am in Christ.

Paul ends chapter 8 by sharing this promise, Romans 8:38–39: "And I am convinced that nothing can ever separate us from God's love. Neither death nor life, neither angels nor demons, neither our fears for today nor our worries about tomorrow—not even the powers of hell can separate us from God's love. No power in the sky above or in the earth below—indeed, nothing in all creation will ever be able to separate us from the love of God that is revealed in Christ Jesus our Lord."

Union with Jesus is everything.

To understand who we are in Christ, we must believe how he sees us. When I embraced the gospel, the miracle of being placed by faith in Christ became my new identity.

In my new relationship with Jesus, his kindness took me entirely by surprise. I embraced him wholeheartedly but felt like I was a constant disappointment to God the Father. I believed he was angry and waiting to discipline me.

For many, the perception of an earthly father and mother can be projected onto our heavenly Father. We do not do this intentionally, but doing so creates an obstacle to trust.

Early in my new identity, I stepped back into a place of sin and struggled with past guilt and shame, striving to believe God could forgive me. I remember lying in bed one night with such a heaviness over me, and I heard God's voice in my spirit, "Ren, I'm on your side."

God spoke volumes to me in that tiny string of words. His words shifted everything. I felt tenderness and compassion pouring from his heart into mine. I was fifty years of age and could finally see God as my loving Father.

The entirety of Psalm 103 is a beautiful reminder of God's kindness and faithfulness. Verses 12–14 are a particular comfort to me during times of insecurity, "He has removed our sins as far from us as the east is from the west. The Lord is like a father to his children, tender and compassionate to those who fear him. For he knows how weak we are: he remembers we are only dust."

CHAPTER SEVENTEEN; CAUGHT IN THE WEB

> The thief's purpose is to steal and kill and destroy. (John 10:10)

Before we moved to Oklahoma, we lived very different lives. We ran a small private feedlot on the eastern plains of Colorado. After we experienced multiple traumatic circumstances, my husband and I decided to move with the last three of our sons to the country. We felt the move would provide a great environment to heal as a family.

We had approximately seventy to eighty customers to whom we provided beef.

The rancher who sold us our home brought in a train car to store his grain. Airtight and perfect for grain storage, the box car was also an excellent breeding ground for spiders. Their magnificent artwork was on display when we opened the door, much like those described in *Charlotte's Web*.

We fed our steers twice daily, at six o'clock a.m. and p.m. I enjoy early mornings, so I took the morning feeding, and our sons took the evening feeding. My husband Dan would head to work, and I would head out to feed the cattle.

We kept a big stick by the door to clear the spider webs before we entered. These webs often took up half the entryway, and I had seen some giant spiders sitting on them.

My husband made sure he described some of the larger ones he'd seen. These stories came from a man who had worked in dark, electrical underground vaults and had been bitten by black widows numerous times. I knew if he thought they were large, they had to be enormous.

One morning, just before daylight, I went out to feed, and for whatever reason, I was distracted. I opened the train car, and without clearing the spider webs, I stepped into the entryway and walked face-first into a giant web. Like a weighted fishing net, the web engulfed me, clinging to my skin.

Let's just say I lost my mind for a few moments, thrashing vigorously, trying to get out of the cobweb. I could visualize one or two spiders clinging to my body somewhere. I can only imagine what I must have looked like. The tension was relieved when I finally emerged, spider-free.

John 10:10 describes the dynamics of the spiritual tension in which we live. "The thief's purpose is to steal and kill and destroy. My purpose is to give them a rich and satisfying life."

Shame is like a spider web, attaching itself to moments in our life journey. We experience times when we frantically try—in our strength and willpower—to remove the web from our lives. Shame is a tool the enemy utilizes to prevent us from experiencing the abundant life Jesus came to give.

To confront shame, we must be clear on what it is and what it is not. Sometimes, we think we're experiencing shame, but what we are feeling is conviction. When we can identify sin in our lives, the conviction of the Holy Spirit encourages us to stop whatever is leading us away from Jesus.

Sometimes, we equate shame with guilt. They are not the same; to be free, we must know the difference. Guilt tells me I have done something terrible or wrong. Shame tells me I am something terrible or wrong; I am flawed; I am bad.

With guilt, we can often ask for forgiveness for something we've done. For example, we can make amends, serve prison time, or pay for a speeding ticket.

But shame sits at the core of our identity. When we allow shame into our lives, it becomes a part of who we are. Whatever we've experienced, whether self-inflicted or at the hands of others, which causes embarrassment and hurt, if left unaddressed, these feelings can evolve into a sense of hopelessness and despair as we frantically try to free ourselves from the web of humiliation. The enemy moves in to kill and destroy hope for the full life Jesus has promised.

In John 4:1–42, we find Jesus's most extended recorded conversation. In this dialogue, we observe him confronting shame. The Pharisees grew concerned about Jesus's popularity, so Christ decided to leave Judea and return to Galilee. Verse 4 reads: "He had to go through Samaria on the way."

The most direct route from Judea to Galilee was seventy miles, or two and a half days, of walking. Because of the conflict between the Jews and the Samaritans, most pious Jews took a longer route to maintain their purity.

The reality is that geographically, Jesus didn't have to go through Samaria. Christ was intentionally going to meet with the Samaritan woman. The latter portion of verse 6 reveals Jesus's humanity. Tired from the journey, he sat down by the well. I believe this also shows his kindness toward the woman. Exhaustion didn't deter Jesus from his mission.

In the heat of the day, this woman approached the well with her water jar. She had three counts against her: she was a Samaritan, a woman, and an outcast. We know she was an outcast because she was alone and hauling water in the hottest part of the day. The well was outside the city, requiring a strenuous walk with large water jars. Fetching water was also a daily social event for women. Since she was alone, we know she was not accepted as a viable part of the community.

Jesus broke all kinds of barriers to capture this woman's heart. In this time and culture, pious Jews did not speak to women in public. Jesus, however, went out of his way to talk with her. Our Lord is displaying radical love.

In Ephesians 1:4, Paul reminds us we have never lived a single second without being loved. "Even before he made the world, God loved us and chose us in Christ to be holy and without fault in his eyes."

As Jesus speaks with the Samaritan woman, the power of love surges through him to reach her. He begins to guide her into an encounter that will transform her life.

In John 4:16–18, Jesus begins to expose her shame. "Go and get your husband,' Jesus told her. 'I don't have a husband,' the woman replied. Jesus said, 'You're right! You don't have a husband—for you have had five husbands, and you aren't even married to the man you're living with now. You certainly spoke the truth!'"

Jesus guided the conversation, and the woman at the well felt safe and fully engaged with him. She didn't lie or run away. Jesus brought her shame into the light.

Brené Brown, a research professor who spent sixteen years studying vulnerability and shame, says regarding shame, "It needs three things to grow exponentially: secrecy, silence, and judgment."[1] Shame cannot survive being spoken. Secrets intensify our shame. When shame is communicated and met with empathy, it begins to lose its power.

Our enemy, Satan, tries to convince us not to express the circumstances surrounding our shame. Humiliation accentuates the possibility of being ridiculed and treated differently. So, we hide our shame instead of exposing it to the light, to the truth of Christ.

Jesus confronted and revealed the shame of the Samaritan woman. He exposed her humiliation to the light and met it with empathy. The pain she carried for years began to lose power over her.

I've often pictured this scene in my mind. When I consider this story, the water jar becomes a focal point of her shame. As the woman approached Jesus, I imagined her positioning the large water container between herself and the Lord. She felt safe behind her jar.

If you've carried humiliation for any length of time, you understand how you can begin to feel comfortable and even secure, hiding behind your shame. To conceal internal struggles, we often create another life to present to the world. We display behavior that isn't congruent with our true selves. We feel safe hiding behind the false life we have created.

In John 4:28–30, we read: "Then, *leaving her water jar*, the woman went back to the town and said to the people, 'Come, see a man who told me everything I ever did.' Could this be the Messiah?' They came out of the town and made their way toward him" (emphasis added).

The Samaritan woman encountered Jesus, and he confronted and exposed her shame. With newfound freedom, she left her jar, shame, and past at her Messiah's feet. She ran to those who had heaped humiliation and offense upon her and told them of his grace.

Thirty-five years ago, I left my water jar at the feet of Jesus. I left my past and shame at the foot of the cross. I continue to run zealously to tell others of his complete forgiveness and amazing grace.

CHAPTER EIGHTEEN: THE SOURCE OF ALL COMFORT

> All praise to God, the Father of our Lord Jesus Christ. God is our merciful Father and the source of all comfort. (2 Corinthians 1:3)

In Paul's letters to the Corinthians, the apostle engages in a dialogue with the Corinthian church. In 1 Corinthians, he addresses specific concerns the church is experiencing, and he offers solutions for these difficulties. In 2 Corinthians, we observe a very different message. Paul gives us a glimpse into his personal life. We learn what he experienced while serving Christ during his trials and sufferings. This great apostle allows himself to be vulnerable to his audience.

False teachers had been attacking Paul's ministry and even his physical appearance. He wrote in 2 Corinthians 10:10, "For some say, 'Paul's letters are demanding and forceful, but in person he is weak, and his speeches are worthless!'"

As a minister of the gospel, I cannot think of any words that could hurt more. These persecuting statements would strike me at the core of my insecurities. To the Corinthian Church, image was important, and Paul seemed to have nothing to offer.

His opponents also questioned Paul's ministry due to the numerous sufferings and trials he had endured. Many still hold onto the idea that if we are faithful followers of Christ, our lives will be devoid of trauma and difficulties. This belief is blatantly incongruent with the Scriptures.

I appreciate that Paul never diminished suffering. He wrote on the topic of comfort in the pages of Scripture more than any other author. Additionally, the apostle addresses suffering more than any other writer. Paul never avoided the subject in his many books, and he often presented his life as an example.

In 2 Corinthians 1:3–7, the concept of comfort or comforting occurs nine times in these five verses: "All praise to God, the Father of our Lord Jesus Christ. God is our merciful Father and the source of all comfort. He comforts us in all our troubles so that we can comfort others. When they are troubled, we will be able to give them the same comfort God has given us. For the more we suffer for Christ, the more God will shower us with his comfort through Christ. Even when we are weighed down with troubles, it is for your comfort and salvation! For when we ourselves are comforted, we will certainly comfort you. Then you can patiently endure the same things we suffer. We are confident that as you share in our sufferings, you will also share in the comfort God gives us."

Since the beginning of time, humans have pursued an intense quest for comfort and ease. We live in a world that is often uncomfortable, and our objective is to make our lives more comfortable.

Throughout history, we have invented machines to perform our hard work, making daily life more efficient and comfortable. Our homes are heated and cooled to make us restful in any season. The cars we drive have all the bells and whistles to promote ease and comfort while driving.

Paul wanted to ensure that the Corinthians understood the comfort he was speaking of was unique to the gospel, extraordinary and superior to any other kind. God provides comfort to his people in times of trials and suffering.

According to this letter, our God is the source of all comfort.

When we experience deep distress, our initial reaction can be to turn to worldly sources of relief. As desperate, hurting people, we search for comfort in food, money, alcohol, sexual gratification, and many other avenues.

Authentic and enduring spiritual comfort comes from God alone.

The goal of this godly respite is not to eliminate our discomfort. The comfort Jesus provides is to support us in our pain, not eliminate the reality of suffering in this life. In my own life, when I have experienced the peace Jesus imparts in times of difficulty, the circumstances surrounding me remained uncomfortable and challenging.

In verse 1:4, Paul repeats that this comfort is all-inclusive. "He comforts us in all our troubles so that we can comfort others. When they are troubled, we will be able to give them the same comfort God has given us."

The "so that" indicates we find purpose and meaning in our pain. God has chosen to work through his people, but we must experience his peace before giving to others.

The heart of God is always to reveal himself to us. Comfort is only meaningful if we have experienced God's gift. We cannot give away something we do not have.

God creates consolers within this process. As our Lord comforts us, we become conduits through which his comfort flows to others. As recipients of God's peace, Paul and his companions were qualified to give to others experiencing difficulty. Receivers become givers, transmitting what originated with God.

In verse 1:6, we get a close-up view of Paul's heart as he shares his trials. "Even when we are weighed down with troubles, it is for your comfort and salvation! For when we ourselves are comforted, we will certainly comfort you. Then you can patiently endure the same things we suffer." Paul believed there was no separation between his life and ministry.

The apostle wanted the Corinthians to understand life was not just about them. Everything we do and experience in life has an eternal impact. Even in his trials and sufferings, Paul believed God was increasing his capacity for ministry and usefulness in advancing the kingdom of Jesus.

As we offer comfort to those in need, we are living out the ultimate pursuit of loving others well. Following Mark 12:28–31, we read in verse 31: "The second is equally important: 'Love your neighbor as yourself.'" Sharing the comfort God first gave you is a radical and intimate display of loving others well.

Several years ago, God gave me a picture of how he uses my story. I saw my life as a painter's palette. On the palette were many different shades and colors, all separated, each one representing various trials and struggles, places of emotional and spiritual pain and suffering, circumstances of sin where Jesus graciously brought freedom, and thoughts to which he had brought wholeness.

On the palette were also several open spaces, leaving room for additional testimony to God's goodness.

When I minister to those around me, whether preaching on a Sunday morning, teaching in a Bible study, or meeting with a friend, I often ask the Holy Spirit which colors God wants to use. Which places of trials, experiences, and areas of redemption does he want me to share? What comfort can I offer?

As I pray and take direction from the Holy Spirit, I move deeper into understanding the greatest commandment. I believe when we make ourselves vulnerable and share our testimony with others, our lives are open to the movement of our Lord. As Jesus's comfort flows through us to those around us, we gain ground in our pursuit of loving God with the totality of our humanity.

When we invest our lives in others, we move away from self-centeredness and closer to the image of Christ.

CHAPTER NINETEEN: THE RIPPLE EFFECT

> Do nothing out of selfish ambition or vain conceit. Rather, in humility, value others above yourselves. (Philippians 2:3 NIV)

I homeschooled my children for fourteen years. Even though I knew God was leading me, I went into this season kicking and screaming. Reflecting on those years, I can now say without hesitation, following God's lead was one of the best decisions for our home. Homeschooling my children was the catalyst for a significant spiritual shift in my legacy personally and for our entire family.

Please hear me. I am not advocating all Christians should homeschool their children. I firmly believe God has a unique plan for every individual family. But this was our journey.

I grew up in a home where education was valued and encouraged. In addition to operating a good-sized farm, my father was a teacher and later transitioned to the position of principal in a local elementary school. My siblings and I grew up knowing we would pursue some form of higher education.

After a late start and with four young sons, I completed my Bachelor of Science in Nursing degree. This was only possible with the support of my incredible husband, in-laws, and sons. My accomplishment was undeniably a family effort.

My degree, combined with a few additional classes, helped me secure the position of special education nurse in a local school district. I worked in this position for five years. The experience provided many opportunities to broaden my knowledge and exposure in the areas of mental health, genetics, the foster-group home arena, abuse, addictions, and much more. I still minister today on the foundation of those early lessons.

Throughout those years, our family experienced a succession of life-altering circumstances. At that time, God began to draw me to the idea of homeschooling our last three sons. Little did I know this undertaking would be a fourteen-year journey.

Jesus's command to love God and love my neighbor intersected in a significant way at this junction in my life. My most rigorous transformation occurred in this sacred season. In the Bible, the word "neighbor" carries a much broader meaning than someone who lives nearby. I have heard neighbor described as someone who is in the ripple effect of your life, a chain of events triggered by the preceding event. This image creates a vivid word picture for me.

When I was a young girl, our farming property included ponds and a river. We would stand on the banks, skip rocks, and see who could throw the farthest. At the point of entry, a cascade of ripples moved outward. As I began to see my life this way, I understood that neighbors encompassed all those in the pathway of my life. Over time, this understanding radically changed my approach to daily living. I wish I could tell you the transformation happened quickly. Truthfully, the awareness of this revelation has taken decades to penetrate my stubborn, prideful, and human heart.

As I began to structure my days to meet our homeschool needs, my self-centeredness was frequently revealed. No matter how much we love our children, they inevitably bring a constant disruption to our personal lives. I was like a stubborn two-year-old trying to hold on to my agenda while making everything else work.

We enter parenthood with fantastic dreams and hopes of shaping and influencing our children for God's kingdom. I believe we can—and are responsible for—moving our children in that direction. I have also learned God has a parallel agenda. The moment a child enters our life, we begin the journey of our most significant season of spiritual growth.

With vulnerability and sincerity, I learned more in the years my children passed through our home than they ever learned from me. I believe this is the way our heavenly Father intended parenthood to be. As we shape and influence our children, God journeys with us and leads us more aggressively toward Christlikeness.

In my parenthood, I have been a mother, a stepmother, an adoptive mother, a mother-in-law, and a grandmother. At each entry point into these precious and privileged stations in life, I have been challenged at the deepest levels of my self-interest.

Recognizing my husband, children (both young and adult), their spouses, and my grandchildren as neighbors has had a profound impact on how I respond in these crucial spaces. If I believe Jesus's implication that neighbors are those we encounter in the pathway of our lives, then my family is the first point of contact.

This understanding requires me to acknowledge my responses to some situations. Even though my intentions were good, they have not always been God-honoring. I have learned we walk the closest with God in those humbling and challenging circumstances. Our spiritual maturing is about progression, not perfection.

I have a picture in my front room that reads, "The most important work you will ever do is within the walls of your home." These words have rich meaning and are profoundly true for every man and woman.

In Luke 10:25–28, we find a conversation between Christ and a holy man. "One day an expert in religious law stood up to test Jesus by asking him this question: 'Teacher, what should I do to inherit eternal life?' Jesus replied, 'What does the law of Moses say? How do you read it?' The man answered, 'You must love the Lord your God with all your heart, all your soul, all your strength, and all your mind. And love your neighbor as yourself.' 'Right!' Jesus told him. 'Do this and you will live!'"

Jesus affirmed the scribe's awareness of the Scriptures. The lawyer's pride and self-righteous character would not allow him to stop at this point, and his next question reveals he did not know how to apply his knowledge. His head knowledge had not yet penetrated his heart. In verse 29, we read, "The man wanted to justify his actions, so he asked Jesus, 'And who is my neighbor?'"

In response to the lawyer's second question, Jesus tells the parable of the good Samaritan (Luke 10:30–37) Perhaps more than any other story, this parable illustrates how our love for God cannot be separated from our love for others. To impact his listeners, Christ addressed a deep cultural hatred present at that time. The story also reveals the depth of our obligation to love others.

Jesus finished the parable with a question. "'Now which of these three would you say was a neighbor to the man who was attacked by bandits?' Jesus asked" (Luke 10:36).

Jesus brilliantly challenged the scribe's question with another question. At this point, the expert in the law must take a quick interpersonal assessment. The conversation shifts and becomes focused not on identifying who the neighbor is but on revealing who acted as a neighbor. The question becomes very personal.

In Luke 10:37, we read, "The man replied, 'The one who showed him mercy.' Then Jesus said, 'Yes, now go and do the same.'" Simply put, doing the right thing is not enough. The command by Jesus is more than a moral duty. Jesus requires us to connect on an emotional level. Christ calls us to respond to those in the pathway of our lives with compassion.

In Romans 15:3, we find a statement impossible for us to imagine: "For even Christ didn't live to please himself." As humans living in a fallen world, most of our lives revolve around pleasing ourselves. Jesus walked out his time on earth differently. Jesus, always our model for living, never allowed his preferences or pride to dictate his decisions in life. Luke 22:42 tells us how Jesus approached one of the most challenging moments in his earthly life: "Father, if you are willing, please take this cup of suffering away from me. Yet I want your will to be done, not mine."

Christ, being fully God and fully man, loved his Father with all aspects of his humanity. In this place of complete love, Jesus stepped into the destiny for which he came to earth. Matthew 20:28 says, "For even the Son of Man came not to be served but to serve others and to give his life as a ransom for many."

The unbroken connection between loving God and loving others reveals itself as Jesus embraces the cross.

CHAPTER TWENTY: THE POWER OF DIGNITY

> Then God said, "Let us make mankind in our image, in our likeness."
> (Genesis 1:26 NIV)

Genesis chapter 1 directly reveals God's decision to create the human race in his image and likeness. In Genesis 1:26, God explains what he is about to do: "Then God said, 'Let us make mankind in our image, in our likeness.'" And then, in 1:27, we read, "So God created humanity in his own image. In the image of God he created them; male and female he created them" (NIV).

We are presented with the incredible knowledge that in all creation, only human beings were made in God's image. Comprehending this foundational concept gives us significance and purpose in life, helping us to understand our inherent dignity as human beings.

Being aware we are God's image bearers profoundly affects our understanding of our relationship with him and creates significant implications for how we treat others. We must grasp the knowledge that we are made in the likeness of our Father, to help us understand how we bear God's image.

God spoke, and the world came into existence. But when God created human beings, he did something different. He formed man from the ground, then the Scriptures tell us he breathed his breath into his handiwork. The man became a living being.

He created the universe, then shaped and formed those who would represent him on earth. He created human beings who could communicate with God, respond to him, and have a relationship with him—a creation to display his character traits.

Adam and Eve were made as spiritual and moral beings. God created them righteous and holy. Our Father's intention has always been that human beings would love him more than anything else, and they would love others well.

In all of creation, Adam and Eve alone could sin, and they did. In Genesis 3, we are confronted with the reality of their sin.

At Adam's fall, God's image in humanity was corrupted, but not destroyed. The result of sin is part of our redemptive story, and the restoration of God's image becomes the predominant pursuit for every believer.

As Christians, our conformity to Christ's likeness is accomplished through redemption. Second Corinthians 3:18 states this beautifully: "So all of us who have had that veil removed can see and reflect the glory of the Lord. And the Lord—who is the Spirit—makes us more and more like him as we are changed into his glorious image."

Complete restoration and perfection of God's image do not happen in this world; they come in the next. Our creator knows we can't be sinless this side of heaven. Throughout the New Testament, Christ continually encourages us to persevere in our spiritual growth.

In Matthew 5:48, in the Sermon on the Mount, Jesus tells the crowd, "But you are to be perfect, even as your Father in heaven is perfect." How do we then resolve Christ's command to be perfect?

The answer lies in the gospel. Jesus is the only one who lived a perfect life. We meet God's standards when we yield our lives to Christ. We cannot earn righteousness. We are declared righteous because of our Savior. Our spiritual salvation requires rebirth into the original moral likeness of God. Colossians 3:10 provides direction for us, "Put on your new nature, and be renewed as you learn to know your Creator and become like him."

In this in-between space, every human is to be treated with dignity and compassion out of respect for the image of God within them. We do not get to choose another person's worthiness; our Creator has predetermined each person's worth.

In Matthew 25:40, Jesus tells us, "Truly I tell you, whatever you did for one of the least of these brothers and sisters of mine, you did for me" (NIV). To love others is to love God himself. The careful attention to these words of Christ creates a radical shift in our perception of others. If we recognize the image of God in our neighbor, we will encounter Jesus in a different way.

This recognition that humans bear the image of God produces a new way of thinking. We begin to understand the immense value of those we meet. We perceive the sacredness of all those who are in the ripple effect of our lives. With this understanding, we can put Jesus's words into practice.

As we step into this place of deep connection between loving God and the image of God, the Scriptures come alive in a fresh way. One such Scripture for me is Ephesians 2:10, which says, "For we are God's handiwork, created in Christ Jesus to do good works, which God prepared in advance for us to do" (NIV).

A few years ago, I had the privilege of caring for my mother-in-law. She lived in our home for ten months until her needs became too great to manage. She spent the last two months of her life in a skilled nursing facility.

Just like parenting, caretaking is never just about meeting the needs of others. God's parallel purpose of making us more like his Son is always at play.

Over that year, my mother-in-law was hospitalized numerous times. One of those hospitalizations required us to call an ambulance to our home. Due to COVID restrictions, the process to allow me to see her took thirty-six hours. When I entered her room, I was confronted with an image I hadn't expected and will never forget.

At ninety, my mother-in-law still took pride in her appearance. She enjoyed simple but pretty clothes. When she lived in our home, I would join her for coffee around 5:30 each morning. She was always dressed: glasses on, hearing aids in, earrings, and wristwatch in place. She topped off her look with beautiful pink lipstick. She was always alert and ready for her day.

But on this morning, I found her sitting in the corner of the semi-darkened hospital room. She wore a disheveled hospital gown and no underwear, glasses, hearing aids, or watch. She had been stripped of all sense of sound, sight, and time.

Her timepiece had given her a sense of safety throughout the past year. We purchased her a watch that recorded the date, days of the week, and time. The watch helped create order in her daily routines. Without that, she was disoriented and confused. Her loss of dignity and respect profoundly affected her.

In that moment, I knew caring for my mother-in-law was one of the good works God had prepared me to do. Among many things, I was called to be her advocate in this season of her life. I was continually confronted with my interests and agendas and didn't always serve her well. But she and

I developed perseverance and a sense of love and respect for one another that marked our relationship for eternity.

When we read Ephesians 2:10, we may imagine the impressive opportunities God created us to accomplish to reflect his kingdom—moments where we are seen and applauded. Though impressive opportunities do occur sometimes, most often God chooses to work in the quiet moments of our ordinary days..

The good works God created us to do, even before we were born, occur as we encounter others in our homes, workplaces, grocery stores, and gyms. Every human being, no matter their age, gender, disability, or standing in life, is due dignity and respect as God's image-bearer.

CHAPTER TWENTY-ONE: THE ADVOCATE

> And I will ask the Father, and he will give you another advocate, who will never leave you.
> (John 14:16)

In the gospel of John, chapters 14 through 16, we find a memorable conversation between Jesus and his disciples the night before he was crucified. Our Lord shared amazing truths with his followers, which sparked fear among the disciples.

These twelve men had been with Christ for three and a half years. They left behind careers, families, and all future aspirations to follow Jesus. The disciples witnessed resurrections, healings, and countless other miracles. The faithful followers experienced deep intimacy as they learned at the feet of the Messiah.

The disciples' lives had become so intertwined with Jesus's life that the idea of his departure would have caused intense distress. Sorrow set in as they began to understand Jesus was preparing to leave them.

I have often reflected on the reality presented in this conversation. Throughout his years with the disciples, Christ implied numerous times a change in their relationship was coming. He made many promises to them about the future. The disciples had created a false concept of the coming kingdom. They imagined that Jesus would establish his kingdom in the physical realm.

However, Christ would fulfill his promises through his departure and death on the cross. His crucifixion would provide eternal life for all who believed in him. I don't think we can fully comprehend the sense of abandonment and hopelessness these devoted men began to experience.

In John 14:1, at what is known as the Last Supper, the Lord addressed their fears and feelings of abandonment. He spoke words of comfort, "Don't let your hearts be troubled. Trust in God, and trust also in me." This is an imperative statement by Jesus, and with the command would come the ability to fulfill the directive.

Then Jesus led them to the core of what he wanted them to understand. He began to open their minds to a new spiritual reality, introducing them to the Holy Spirit.

In John 14:15–17, we read, "If you love me, obey my commandments. And I will ask the Father, and he will give you another advocate, who will never leave you. He is the Holy Spirit, who leads into all truth. The world cannot receive him, because it isn't looking for him and doesn't recognize him. But you know him, because he lives with you now and later *will be in you*" (emphasis added).

The word "advocate" is not often used in our daily language. In other translations, the original Greek word "parakletos" is translated as counselor, comforter, encourager, and helper, meaning "one called alongside to help." This reveals to us the many aspects of the work and ministry of the Holy Spirit.

We cannot overlook the word "another," placed right before the word advocate. The Greek word for "another" is "allos," meaning "another of the same kind." This placement of words helps broaden our understanding of what Jesus is saying. He indicates to his disciples, like Jesus, the Holy Spirit is also God.

Christ has been their advocate and helper. He has physically been with them. When he is gone, the Holy Spirit will come and dwell in them to continue Jesus's work.

God's intentions were never for us to walk out our Christian journey without support and guidance. Christ knew we, as believers, would face many difficulties in this world. In John 14:18, Jesus gave the disciples (and us) a radical promise filled with tenderness and love. "No, I will not abandon you as orphans—I will come to you."

Jesus's language is direct and carefully chosen. Christ is within hours of his crucifixion; his heart is filled with concern and affection for his disciples. In my journey as a nurse and provider of pastoral care, as well as in my personal life, I have found near-death conversations are concise and filled with raw truth. Here, the Messiah used language that is direct and penetrates the heart.

In one word, Christ identifies the depth of their abandonment. The word "orphan" means fatherless children. He reassures them his leaving would not be the devastating disaster they were feeling and imagining.

When we give our lives to Christ, the Holy Spirit comes within us and identifies us as God's children. Romans 8:16 says, "For his Spirit joins with our spirit to affirm that we are God's children." If you have accepted Jesus's offer of salvation, at no time since you committed your life to Christ have you ever been alone. Jesus's very words in John 14:16 confirm this truth: "He will give you another Advocate who will never leave you." We have the assurance of the continual indwelling presence of the Holy Spirit.

At the peak of the COVID pandemic, these words in Scripture brought me great comfort. As a care pastor, part of my responsibility was to visit our church family who were in the hospital or care facilities, or those who were unable to leave home due to health reasons. I experienced intimate depths of friendship and love as I ministered to those who were ill.

Due to COVID restrictions, I was unable to visit and sit at the bedside of a precious couple who died months apart. In a particular moment of deep sadness at the thought of not being with them, the Spirit reminded me of John 14:16.

I had walked with this couple for several years and knew the Holy Spirit abided in them. Through this reminder, I knew the God of all comfort and the greatest encourager was with them in the moments leading up to their departure. I knew the Advocate, the very Spirit of God, would remind them of all the fulfilled promises that awaited them. John 14:26, "But when the Father sends the Advocate as my representative—that is, the Holy Spirit—he will teach you everything and will remind you of everything I have told you."

The Spirit is the third member of the Trinity: God the Father, God the Son, and God the Holy Spirit. Though the word trinity is not found in the Bible, the truth it represents flows throughout the Scriptures:

- "And I will ask the Father, and he will give you another Advocate, who will never leave you." (John 14:16)
- "But when the Father sends the Advocate as my representative—that is, the Holy Spirit—he will teach you everything and will remind you of everything I have told you." (John 14:26)
- "and the Holy Spirit, in bodily form, descended on him like a dove. And a voice from heaven said, 'You are my dearly loved Son, and you bring me great joy.'" (Luke 3:22)
- "But I will send you the Advocate—the Spirit of truth. He will come to you from the Father and will testify all about me." (John 15:26)

These Scriptures provide clarifying evidence the Holy Spirit is an equal member of the Trinity. He is as much God as the person of the Father and of the Son.

The Bible identifies the Holy Spirit in various ways, each description revealing that the Holy Spirit is God himself.

- "The earth was formless and empty, and darkness covered the deep waters. And the Spirit of God was hovering over the surface of the waters" (Genesis 1:2).
- "Then, coming to the borders of Mysia, they headed north for the province of Bithynia, but again, the Spirit of Jesus did not allow them to go there" (Acts 16:7).
- "And because we are his children, God has sent the Spirit of his Son into our hearts, prompting us to call out, 'Abba, Father'" (Galatians 4:6).
- "God himself has prepared us for this, and as a guarantee, he has given us his Holy Spirit" (2 Corinthians 5:5).

In the private and intimate conversation found in John 14, Christ reveals the coming of the Holy Spirit. Jesus knew the presence of the Spirit was necessary for the disciples to comprehend their new reality. The invaluable truth the Lord Jesus imparted to his followers that evening, so many years ago, is still just as relevant for you and me today.

To live a victorious Christian life, we need the presence of the Holy Spirit. His work, power, and ministry are necessities to help us reach the finish line.

CHAPTER TWENTY-TWO: THE FELLOWSHIP OF THE HOLY SPIRIT

> May the grace of the Lord Jesus Christ, the love of God, and the fellowship of the Holy Spirit be with you all. (2 Corinthians 13:14)

Our relationship with the Holy Spirit is essential to our Christian journey. We must understand there is no salvation without the ministry of the Holy Spirit. All transformed hearts and lives are the work of the Spirit. The Scriptures counsel us on this vital truth.

- 2 Thessalonians 2:13, "As for us, we can't help but thank God for you, dear brothers and sisters loved by the Lord. We are always thankful that God chose you to be among the first to experience salvation—a salvation that came through the Spirit who makes you holy and through your belief in the truth."
- John 6:63, "The Spirit alone gives eternal life. Human effort accomplishes nothing. And the very words I have spoken to you are spirit and life."

In John chapters 14, 15, and 16, Jesus discloses to his disciples the transition that is taking place. These chapters contain Jesus's last significant teaching. In this section of

Scripture, Christ encourages us to welcome and embrace the Holy Spirit.

The disciples became anxious as they began to comprehend some of what Jesus was sharing with them. He was preparing to leave them. Our Lord's crucifixion and death were just hours away. He would soon physically ascend to heaven. He would not abandon them but leave them in the care of the Holy Spirit.

Jesus was physically present with his disciples for three years, but the Holy Spirit would come and dwell inside them after his death, resurrection, and ascension into heaven. Again, Scripture defines the plan.

- John 16:7: "It is best for you that I go away, because if I don't, the Advocate won't come. If I do go away, then I will send him to you."
- 1 Corinthians 3:16, "Don't you know that you yourselves are God's temple and that God's Spirit dwells in your midst?" (NIV).

We often rush past the words in John 16:7, missing the profound emotions and confusion evoked by Jesus's words. The disciples could physically touch and see Christ. They could look into his face, observe his feelings, see his hand gestures, and ask him questions. Without the indwelling of the Holy Spirit, they could not see the advantage of Jesus leaving.

As believers, Christ lives in us through the person of the Holy Spirit. At the moment of salvation, God's Spirit abides in us as the continual presence of Jesus. Titus 3:5–6 illustrates a concise picture of this plan. "He saved us, not because of the righteous things we had done, but because of his mercy. He washed away our sins, giving us a new birth and new life through the Holy Spirit. He generously poured out the Spirit upon us through Jesus Christ our Savior."

When we are born again, a portion of the Spirit's ministry is to make us aware of Christ in us, not in the omnipresent way (being everywhere simultaneously), but in a personal, real-time way. The fellowship of the Holy Spirit begins at salvation and remains throughout our lives and into eternity.

As the Holy Spirit lives within us, he brings life-changing results.

One of the initial differences I experienced at salvation was an intense energy for living: a zest for life. My days were filled with meaning and purpose as I looked toward the future. John 6:63 testifies to this: "The Spirit gives life; the flesh counts for nothing. The words I have spoken to you—they are full of the Spirit and life" (NIV).

The Spirit of God generates hope. We find this in Romans 15:13, "I pray that God, the source of hope, will fill you completely with joy and peace because you trust in him. Then you will overflow with confident hope through the power of the Holy Spirit."

The indwelling of the Holy Spirit places the new believer into the body of Christ, his universal church. First Corinthians 12:13 sheds light on this truth: "But we have all been baptized into one body by one Spirit, and we all share the same Spirit."

The Holy Spirit teaches us. He interprets the words of Jesus concerning the world and the circumstances in which we live. John 14:26 points to this vital truth: "But when the Father sends the Advocate as my representative—that is, the Holy Spirit—he will teach you everything and will remind you of everything I have told you."

We build our lives on the decisions we make. The Holy Spirit will guide us into the truth of our choices, providing direction in both small and big decisions. We find this encouragement in John 16:13, "When the Spirit of truth comes, he will guide you into all truth. He will not speak on his own but will tell you what he has heard. He will tell you about the future."

The Spirit gives evidence of our new life as the fruit becomes visible. Galatians 5:22 teaches us, "But the Holy Spirit produces this kind of fruit in our lives: love, joy, peace, patience, kindness, goodness, faithfulness, gentleness, and self-control."

The Holy Spirit empowers us to live in accordance with God's will for our lives. We find this promise in Galatians 5:15: "So I say, let the Holy Spirit guide your lives. Then you won't be doing what your sinful nature craves."

At the moment of salvation, our destination is no longer undetermined. Rebirth from above establishes the trajectory of our lives. Encountering difficulties on our journey is inevitable, but our Creator, God, has ensured we reach the finish line. The Holy Spirit supplies us with the power, energy, wisdom, and divine purpose to pursue loving God and loving others, bringing us closer to the image of Christ.

As we develop our relationship with the Spirit and are willing to seek his help, he will support us in every moment of our lives. We can be confident the Holy Spirit will bring us across the finish line all the way home.

However, we must first be in the race. I need to ask, have you stepped off the starting block? Have you received Christ's gift of salvation? According to Jesus's words in John 3:3, we must be spiritually reborn to see the kingdom of God.

Later in John 14:6, Christ gives us clear directions on how to enter the race. "I am the way, the truth, and the life. No one comes to the Father except through me" (NIV).

Christ is "the way" to God the Father. He is not one of many ways—he is the only path to God. Jesus, God's perfect son, was the only one who could provide access to a relationship with our creator. He gave us the way out of our spiritual darkness.

This understanding was not a popular position in the days of Christ, and is often rejected today. The gospel appears too simplistic to many in our world. Many believe there should be other paths to God. These paths entail hard work and striving, indicating that the accomplishment of eternal life is something to be earned. Paul dismantles this belief in Ephesians 2:9: "Salvation is not a reward for the good things we have done, so none of us can boast about it."

The reality lies in Jesus's own words. The only way to have a relationship with God our Father is through faith in Jesus Christ alone.

Understanding Jesus is the only way has brought so much freedom into my life. I was in the shadow of the Pharisee when he asked Christ which was the greatest commandment. The regulations and rules that surrounded me the night of May 21, 1990, were unattainable. They left me exhausted from striving and hopeless of ever achieving the forgiveness I longed for.

The letter of the law was not intended to guide us in achieving salvation. Christ created the law to point us to him. Only in Jesus could I receive forgiveness and the gift of eternal life.

I didn't recite a sinner's prayer, and I didn't walk an aisle. I had an honest conversation with my God. I had always known Christ had died for my sins, but I believed the path to forgiveness was Jesus plus something else.

No one needed to tell me I was a sinner. I knew I had failed God on many levels. I expressed my sorrow to him and asked for his help. I wanted to live a better life and give my sons a new legacy. I surrendered my life to Jesus.

Since that time, with the help of his Spirit, loving God with all my human capability has become the ultimate pursuit of my life. I don't always do it well, but because of the mercy and kindness of Jesus Christ, and the help and encouragement of the Spirit, I keep my running shoes on. I have learned as he matures me, stretches me, disciplines me, and imparts his love to me, I have many new areas to offer him.

If you feel dissatisfied with your life, or if you wonder why you don't see more personal growth or experience more peace, I understand. For you, life may always feel difficult and exhausting. I encourage you to reach out to Jesus and have an honest conversation about your life. He won't disappoint you.

As we close our time together, let me share some comforting words from Scripture. Second Peter 3:9 says, "The Lord is not slow in keeping his promise, as some understand slowness. Instead, he is patient with you, not wanting anyone to perish, but everyone to come to repentance" (NIV).

This can be your moment.

As you surrender your life to Christ, God will fulfill his promise and send the Holy Spirit to dwell in you. He will give you all the support you need to cross the finish line and to hear Christ say, "Well done, my good and faithful servant" (Matthew 25:21 NIV).

ABOUT THE AUTHOR

Renny Bailey holds a Bachelor of Science in Nursing, which has allowed her many diverse experiences. She continues to draw on these skills in caring for those she ministers to. In addition to five years as a special education nurse, Bailey has served in a variety of ministries, including as a staff pastor, women's ministry leader, and conference speaker, including in Cambodia and Zambia. Bailey and her husband Dan joined their families thirty-four years ago and have six children and fourteen grandchildren.

ENDNOTES

Chapter One

Stephen Covey, *The Seven Habits of Highly Effective People* (Simon and Schuster, 1990).

Chapter Three

Juliann Scholl, "When Should You Take the ACT? Test Dates: Best Colleges." BestColleges.com, 2022. https://www.bestcolleges.com/blog/when-to-take-act/.

Chapter Six

Mike Petzer, *The Gospel of Identity* (pub by author, 2014), 11.

Chapter Eight

C. S. Lewis, *Mere Christianity* (Harper Collins Publishers, 2001), 158–159.

Ibid., 147.

Chapter Nine

Merriam-Webster Dictionary, "legacy," accessed November 19, 2022, https://www.merriam-webster.com/.

Chapter Ten

Merriam-Webster Dictionary, "endurance," March 15, 2023, https://www.merriam-webster.com/.

Kay Warren, *Choose Joy: Because Happiness Isn't Enough* (Baker Publishing Group, 2012), 27.

"Cultivating a Life of Worship and Joy," Renovaré, 2002. https://renovare.org/articles/cultivating-a-life-of-worship.

Chapter Sixteen

John R.W Stott, "'In Christ': The Meaning and Implications of the Gospel of Jesus Christ." C. S. Lewis Institute, June 3, 2007, https://www.cslewisinstitute.org/resources/in-christ-the-meaning-and-implications-of-the-gospel-of-jesus-christ/.

Chapter Seventeen

Brené Brown, "Listening to Shame," TED Talk, March 2012, 20 min., 38 sec., https://youtu.be/psN1DORYYVo?si=a5MY6_K2AqFCK-wO.

Made in the USA
Las Vegas, NV
11 December 2025

36227653R00085